Dedicated to
ZIG ZIGLAR
1926 - 2012

He helped me and so many others
to build our lives.

LIFE
BUILDERS
Stories That Inspire

2016

Copyright © 2016
Mike Rodriguez International
Frisco, Texas

Tribute Publishing

Life Builders
First Edition February 2016

All Worldwide Rights Reserved
ISBN: 978-0-9906001-7-6

All Rights Reserved. No part of this book may be reproduced, stored in a retrieval system, or transmitted, in any form, or by any means, electronic, mechanical, recorded, photocopied, or otherwise, without the prior written permission of the copyright owner, except by a reviewer who may quote brief passages in a review.

Printed in the United States of America.

In God We Trust

> "Changing the world starts with changing your own life."
> Mike Rodriguez

Contents

Prologue xi

Chapter 1 – A Simple Decision 1

Chapter 2 – The Benefit of the Benefit 11

Chapter 3 – Growth Has No Stop-Date 25

Chapter 4 – A Working Definition 39

Chapter 5 – The Warrior Who Painted Her Fight 51

Chapter 6 – What Are You Thinking 77

Chapter 7 – Start by Changing Yourself 95

Chapter 8 – Overcoming Adversity 107

Chapter 9 – Manifest Magnificence 119

Epilogue 135

About Mike Rodriguez 137

x

Prologue

I decided to publish this book because I knew there were others like me who had a story to tell. Others that had faced major challenges they had overcome. Other normal people like me and like you that had a story to share or who just needed their voice to be heard.

The contributing Authors in this book were brave enough to share their own thoughts, stories and insights. They did this with the hopes that other people, like you, would find something to take away. Something that would inspire others to make the important changes in their own lives. To understand that what you are going through does not define you, but can certainly refine you to start building your best life. You can do it, however, you must be willing to believe, to take action, and to start pursuing your greatest purpose to change your life. I would like to tell you that it is going to be easy, but it is not. I would like to say that there is nothing special about the contributors to this book, but that would also not be true. Yet, it would also be false for you to believe that there is nothing special about you, too. You were created with precision, purpose, and your own unique talents. You were also given the ability to know, act on, and use those talents to become great and strong in your own way. Just know, remember, and most importantly believe this, "I can do all things through Christ, who strengthens me." Philippians 4:13 (*NKJV*). Through faith and action, ALL things are possible.

Now let's get started on building your life.

"I am still stretching and growing like a little baby. My graduation day for growth has not arrived. The days that have passed on the calendar, few or many, do not give me a license to sit down and fold my hands, but rather to keep on reaching.
Today this makes very little sense whatsoever.
A year from now I'll wish I had started today."

Marie Calberry

Chapter 1

A Simple Decision
By Mike Rodriguez

You never know how the words you share might impact another life. Words inspire thought. Thought leads to inspiration and inspiration to decisions. Decisions can be simple, but they must be influenced by inspiration.

When I was in high school, I decided to choose an art class as an easy way to complete my schedule. At that time, I was coasting along in my life, ready to graduate, but without direction. Sure I was told by many that I needed to start thinking about my future, but I wasn't buying it. People simply cannot think about something we don't believe in.

I felt that I should do something with my life, I just didn't know how or what to do. Sadly, I didn't know why I should do anything either. It was like my life compass was broken and I just couldn't find a way to get to where I needed to go. As a result, I wasn't making any decisions.

Greatness can be found inside of each of us. With some, it might be found buried very deep inside, but it is still inside.

With others, the false belief that their greatness doesn't even exist is powerful enough to keep them from even considering that they have greatness.

Chapter 1 – A Simple Decision

Consider your life and your purpose to be equivalent to mining a diamond. In its easiest description, you must work extremely hard at removing a great deal of dirty and worthless carbon to uncover the shine and value of the jewel that is inside.

From a more complicated perspective, and with a touch of reality, you have to first believe that a diamond can even be found. You must believe so you can decide to take action. Then, your belief must be strong enough to keep pushing you each day as you work and work without seeing any progress. Next you must re-engage with yourself, daily, to be persistent. You must understand the benefit to you and everyone else involved once you find that magnificent treasure.

> *"Too many of us never get started and many others quit when things get too tough."*
> *Mike Rodriguez*

All of these things work together to ensure that you will see and continue to realize the big picture for your life.

If your belief in *you* isn't strong enough, two things will happen: First, you might not even decide to get started to begin with. Secondly, if you do begin, but your purpose isn't deep enough, you will decide to quit when things get too tough.

Chapter 1 – A Simple Decision

So there I was in this art class, just existing, without identifying any purpose, belief or direction. That is until one day during the final week of the year.

My art teacher, an interesting and inspiring lady, called me over at the end of the class. She proceeded to give me a paper. I put it in my folder, smiled at her and went on my way to complete my day.

When I arrived home after school, my mother was going through my folder and found the paper. She called me in and read it to me. My teacher had written a revised quote by Henry David Thoreau:

> To Mike,
> "You have built castles in the air,
> and your work need not be lost;
> that is where they should be.
> Now put the foundations under them."

My mind starting thinking. Did she see something in me? Had I built castles in the air? Looking back, the biggest thing I took away was that the decision to even start building my dreams was completely up to me.

Something happened. I was motivated and I could start to feel direction. Those words inspired thought. Yes, I was capable of building foundations for my castles in the air. I wanted to and I felt I could.

I didn't know that those few simple words written years ago for anyone, but shared with me, would have such a profound effect on my life. Simple words that would inspire me to decide to take action. Something stood out to me: Dreams must have foundations built under them. Without the proper

Chapter 1 – A Simple Decision

foundation, dreams cannot be built. This is another complicated part of life, as your foundation is built on the solid things that you do. These are the actions that generate the results that inevitably impact your life.

I would like to tell you that I started changing my life immediately, but I didn't. What I can tell you is that a new seed of thought had been planted in my mind. This would be a powerful seed that would continue to grow as I would grow: The power to decide.

An additional contributing factor to my personal growth has also been my parents. Both of my parents weren't raised wealthy. As a result, they learned early on to appreciate the value of life and their relationships over material possessions. That mindset carried over to their actions as parents. Both of them told me many stories about when they were growing up. At an early age, my father recognized his desire to excel. This was instilled by his mother who was a very strong and influential person in his life. She was an intelligent woman, even though she had only attended school up through third grade. His father had attended up through 4th grade. As a child, it would have been easy for my father to believe that he had those same limitations. He could have easily let those limitations hold him back. Instead, the discipline and work ethic instilled in him by his parents created a driving force inside of him.

This same man who pushed and continues to push me and my brothers and sisters to work hard and pursue our dreams, is the same man who used to sell bananas on the streets when he was only 12 years old. It's tough to argue with that. Sure you could say times are different, but I would disagree.

Chapter 1 – A Simple Decision

We should all still be inspired enough to make the right decisions to change our lives.

For my father, he attended school for half a day, then the other half his mother encouraged him to work. I would like to say it was primarily to earn income, but his profits actually went to his mother. His mother wanted to instill work ethic, purpose and value in him. Later, at the same age of 12, he worked on the streets as a bus ticket taker.

As he grew up, my father was aware that his friends were either joining gangs, going to prison or just dying early. This wasn't for him. When he was about 19 years old, he was drafted into the Army. He hardly spoke English and had a hard time communicating. Because of this, people incorrectly assumed he was ignorant and they harassed him. My dad, a resilient man, completed his two years of service and left to start his life.

As all great stories go, mine included, my father met the love of his life several years later. I would like to say it's as simple as that, but it isn't. You must know that for a white woman, my mother, to date a minority during that period of time was not accepted, socially or other. When you partner that with the fact that my father primarily only spoke Spanish and my mother spoke English, it was a recipe for failure. My mother didn't see it that way. She saw purpose in this man and she made a decision to marry him. He would find new motivation in caring for his family, by working 18 hours a day as a cab driver.

One day a turn of events happened. Their first child, my oldest brother Anthony, became very sick.

Chapter 1 – A Simple Decision

Thankfully my father had his cab as transportation and rushed Anthony to the hospital. This situation left my father feeling vulnerable and concerned. He was now motivated and inspired to take action. As a result, my mother and my father talked about their life plans.

Together they gathered their facts. They knew what was best and they made a new decision. At the age of 27, my father would go back into the Army. This meant that he would be away from his family and children for extended periods of time. This also meant that my mother would be alone caring for our family. However, everyone would have health benefits. My parents experienced powerful motivation and sacrifice to make a simple decision.

As an enlisted man in the U.S. Army, my father put his work ethic and integrity into action. One day his battalion commander approached him and encouraged him to apply for warrant officer school. This would be a big step for my father, a giant move for his career and would have a tremendous impact on his family. My father's confidence was low. He didn't have the college education and he could hardly speak English. He didn't think he would get accepted, so he let his emotions override his passion and he decided not to pursue the challenge. He made a decision and said no. Unfortunately, my father could not see what his battalion commander saw in him.

A few days later, this same colonel called my Dad into his office. The colonel had completed the application for my father to apply. My dad was shocked, but he was also inspired because this man believed in him. The colonel handed my father the application and asked him to sign it.

Chapter 1 – A Simple Decision

My dad was now facing another turning point in his life that would be altered by a simple decision. This time, his purpose was strong and he could see a future. He decided he would go for it and he made a decision to sign the papers.

After a period of time, and to my father's surprise, he was called before a selection board for an extensive interview. When he finished the interview, he wasn't sure of the outcome. He was nervous and hoped for the best, but to him, the outlook didn't look good. It took a period of time, but the day arrived and he received the written notification. As he read it, he was overwhelmed. He was accepted.
He was now going to be a Warrant Officer. His decision would have a profound impact on his life and on his family.

Through his decades of military service, he would continue to make many sacrifices for our country and for our family. He was away from us for extended periods of time, including being away to fight in the Vietnam War.

Because of my father's experience and his value to the U.S. Army, my father would go on to be selected to serve as a U.S. military advisor to the Honduran Government. The same young man who was raised without many material possessions, but with great discipline; who once sold bananas and would later drive a cab to support his family, had now attained the rank of Chief Warrant Officer 4.

My father stayed in the U.S. Army until he retired at the age of 62. He would have stayed longer, but he was required to retire due to the Army's age limit.

Chapter 1 – A Simple Decision

Looking back, there were times when I don't know how my mother kept our family of five kids running. She is also a true hero and an inspiration to me. As I write this book, my parents are retired and live comfortably and happy.

It does make you think, none of the key major events of their lives would have happened if they had not made their decisions. They looked in their hearts during these critical points and they took action. The act of making a decision is quite simple, but I must also tell you this: if you are living your life and you believe that you are not ready to make a key decision, then you must understand that you have already made a decision. You have decided not to take action. With this, you need to know that life teaches us that you will lose much more by not making a decision, than by making the wrong decision.

As I started out telling you, everyone faces challenges. To overcome your challenges, you must dream, motivate yourself and believe in who you are. You must know that the life you are living can become greater than what you are realizing. Then, once you get to that point in your life, the point of inspiration to take action, you will know it. That is the time to simply make a decision to do what you need to do.

Push all fear aside, find your strength and remember this: you only need to start by making your simple decision. That's it and the rest will follow as you build your life to new heights. You might say, well Mike my decisions aren't simple. I would tell you that you are fooling yourself.

Chapter 1 – A Simple Decision

What simple decision will you make today to impact your life?

Now go forth and make your life exceptional!

- By Mike Rodriguez

"The only true limitations you will have
are the ones that you accept and believe."
Mike Rodriguez

Chapter 1 – A Simple Decision

Chapter 2

The Benefit of the Benefit
By Tracy D. Day

America's Motivator, Zig Ziglar, once said on the subject of self-image, "Man was designed for accomplishment, engineered for success, and endowed with the seeds of greatness." This book is a collection of encouraging stories to assist you. Stories to cultivate your mindset that you are endowed with the seeds of greatness. You do have good things inside you no matter who you are, where you were raised, or your current circumstances. I encourage you to be the person you were meant to be, to do the things you are supposed to do and have all the success you have earned. In addition, you already know that a positive change in your mindset and behavior will reap positive benefits, I would like for you to think beyond just the initial benefit. Ponder and consider and understand the benefit of the benefit. Think just beyond yourself and the initial benefit to you.

The old adage, "they must have been born with a silver spoon" refers to those who were born into wealth or what society deems the good life. However, others are born into this world just like any other child to a normal life. So what makes the difference between two children who were born on the same day under similar circumstances? Let the debating begin.

Chapter 2 – The Benefit of the Benefit

An infant child, Travis, was born addicted to drugs in a relatively small town in Texas. He was a tiny boy barely larger than a grown man's shoe. He weighed only 5 pounds and 7 oz. and a long 13 inches. A tiny child, he was off to a rough start. The doctors could tell immediately that this child was a fighter. He was immediately placed into foster care with a young couple. That couple gave the child love and hope. He was surrounded by a family that loved him and encouraged him. His life grew to be like any other child who grew up in a small town. It had ups and it had downs. He had a burning desire deep within him that he could be anything he wanted to be, do anything he wanted to do, and he could have anything he wanted to have through hard work and dedication to his dreams.

Despite his troubling start, he began to grow physically and mentally. His mindset was changing. He began to feed his mind with positive affirmations. As you continue to read, hopefully, you will see the transformation in Travis, just as I hope you will transform into becoming the person you want to be, or more importantly, the person you are supposed to become – the one to serve your purpose.

I mentioned Zig Ziglar earlier in the chapter. I was taught at an early age by my dad, Zig's principles of Be, Do, and Have. Let's jump right into these great Zig Ziglar principles that have inspired millions of people.

BE
So what was it that began the change in Travis?

Chapter 2 – The Benefit of the Benefit

Someone told him that he was important and that he was going to be successful. He had the raw talent to become anyone he wanted to be and do anything he wanted to do. He was encouraged by one of his high school teachers. She was the only one who saw the good in him. She saw though the pain of him finding out he was adopted, and his perception that he wasn't loved or wanted. Never mind the fact that a loving couple adopted him and gave him a new, better life. He grew to understand the love they gave him.

His teacher began to speak positively into his life. She began to challenge him, encourage him, and teach him not only on HOW to do things, or WHAT to do, but most importantly she showed him WHY.

Simon Sinek gave a great TED talk on how great leaders inspire action. In his talk he spoke on the "Golden Circle." Think of it like a target with the bullseye right the middle. Starting from the outside and working your way to the bullseye is: What, How and Why.

Simon explained that is the normal method for most people and organizations. He then continues to give examples of great organizations and individuals who started from the inside out – Why, How and What. He talked about Dr. Martin Luther King, Jr., the Wright brothers, and the Apple Corporation. This is what I encourage you to do.

I encourage you to discover your why. What motivates you? This is the beginning of being the right person you are destined to be. What motivates you? What gets your motor running every morning? What is the reason you are alive?

Chapter 2 – The Benefit of the Benefit

Once you discover your WHY, everything else will begin to fall into place.

Zig Ziglar told a story about him meeting a lady at the request of an associate. This lady spoke of having work relationship issues at her place of employment and was looking for Zig to solve all her problems. The lady complained about her job and all those negative people down there. After a few minutes of talking, he finally had her writing down all the positives of her job and her life. He instructed her to write, "I like my job because _____."

She was to repeat each item every morning in front of the mirror with energy and enthusiasm. He concluded that within 30 days, change "I like" to "I love" and repeat daily from then on. Although the lady didn't know it, Zig was teaching her to be the best she could be, be the right person, and be the example, not the problem.

As the story goes, Zig met that lady again a few months later and she simply said, "Zig, you will not believe how much those folks down at my job changed. I love working there." We all recognize that those people didn't change, she did. You become that person, you make that internal shift.

Some would say that when you find your why, you will be the person you need to be. I think differently. Be the person you need to be and your why will reveal itself. Let me explain it this way: When an egg breaks by outside forces, life ends. When an egg is broken by internal forces, life begins. The same is true with us. Your life begins to get better when you make the decision for a better life and act upon that decision.

Chapter 2 – The Benefit of the Benefit

Travis began his transformation to be the best he could be. He began to see and act differently.

<u>The Benefit of the Benefit:</u> BE the positive person you are destined to be and everyone around you will grow and develop into what they are supposed to be. It is a win-win for everyone you come in contact with on a daily basis.

DO

The question remains – What makes one person succeed more than another? I think the answer, in part, is education, attitude, and most importantly choice. Education is a given. We have all heard that we are supposed to graduate high school, go to college, and get a great job. Some kids are told that they WILL attend a particular college or university because of its prestige. The key here is no matter where you attend college or university, you still obtain something of value – an education. Knowledge is more than a formal education at a higher learning institution.

"Knowledge is power" has been stated through the generations. I would add to the statement, "Applied knowledge is power." We can have all the information we want or need, but if we don't apply that knowledge, then the knowledge's value has diminished.

Wisdom is obtained through experience. As we go through life, we sometimes feel like the battle will never end and we are trapped within our own rut. The negative cycle seems to never stop. As you begin to gain an understanding that a positive mindset and your choice to become better will improve your situation, you start to see that this new knowledge applied with positive action becomes power.

Chapter 2 – The Benefit of the Benefit

Power to change and improve your situation and become the person you chose to be. However, having the knowledge and doing nothing about it, can leave you in a worse situation than you were in before.

Travis was told a story about a man who was lost in the desert for days. The rescue team found the man and got him to safety. As he sat there looking at a nice, cool glass of water he stated, "I believe that if I drink this glass of water, I will live." The man repeated his statement again and again, "I believe that if I drink this glass of water, I will live."
He died sitting in the chair.

He had the knowledge, he had the power to act on that knowledge but did nothing. He did not put his knowledge into action.

Apply some or all of the positive actions that are contained within this book. One suggestion I encourage you to do is the same as what Zig told that lady: Write down all the positive things in your life. Print them on a sheet of paper and place them on your mirror in your bathroom. Say each morning with power and conviction each of the positive things in your life – "I like ____ because ____." Within the first 30 days, you should feel different and begin to change "I like" to "I love." You do the same, change "I like" to "I love" and do so every day.

As you change, grow, and develop, feel free to rework your list, but do not stop your daily affirmation.

Chapter 2 – The Benefit of the Benefit

Apply this affirmation knowledge and act on that knowledge. Do the work. Do what you know that needs to be accomplished.

Society has a way of placing labels on people and people accept that label. In my mind, too many people have no idea of what value they can bring to themselves and the world around them. They have been told for so long what they CAN'T do vs being told what they CAN do. They don't know what they want because their dreams and goals have been taken from them before they had time to be planted and grown. Every person is a different type of flower, and collectively, we make such a beautiful garden.

If you don't like who you are and where you are today, be encouraged because you are not stuck where you are. You can grow to become more than you are today. You can change and become that successful person you have dreamed of becoming today. You can be that phenomenal person.
Your journey begins today!

The movie trilogy, *The Matrix*, climaxed in the third movie in a battle between the main two characters. Neo, who is known as "The One," learns that his opposite is Mr. Smith. Mr. Smith is replicating himself like a computer virus to take over Zion, the last remaining city and more. As the scene plays out, finally Mr. Smith asks, "Why? Why do you persist?"

Chapter 2 – The Benefit of the Benefit

Neo, who is hurt and struggling to stay alive, looks Mr. Smith in the eyes and calmly responds, "Because I choose to." Your journey begins today, by your choice!

Choose to be, do, and have more.

Jim Rohn famously said, "Don't wish your circumstances were different, wish you were better!"

Negative people complain about what is happening to them, instead of doing something about it. They choose not to fight, as it is easier to complain than to improve. It is easier to post something negative on social media and blindly hide behind their phone or tablet than it is to challenge themselves to become better. Granted, your life will not improve overnight, but it will change with the right choices. It will be better for you. Everything you do comes down to choice. Everything. Some people would argue that they didn't choose to live where they live, work where they work, or drive the car they drive. They wanted something different or better. It is possible that is true, it is also possible because of financial situations. It is also true that they can make a choice to be, do, and have more.

When Zig Ziglar would speak to his audiences, he would begin with a question, "How many of you, within the next 10 days, believe that there is something you can directly do to make your personal life, business life, and spiritual life WORSE?" Now, of course, the audience would ripple with laughter and giggles. He would then ask, "How many of you, within the next 10 days, believe that there is something you

Chapter 2 – The Benefit of the Benefit

can directly do to make your personal life, business life, and spiritual life BETTER?" Hands would go up, heads would nod in agreement, and murmurs of agreement would carry through the seats. Zig would then verbally and emotionally grab them with a statement that the audience had not realized he had just revealed to them, "Folks, you have the power to make your life better or worse… and… the… choice… is… yours."

I encourage you to make that choice to be better. You are worth it. Your life does have meaning and value. I firmly believe that every person has a purpose. Just as you have a purpose, Travis had a purpose as well. He began to grow into his own and developed a servant leadership mentality. He started reading all the positive mental attitude books he could get his hands on. Some were loaned to him by friends and mentors, others he bought. I suggest you do the same as well. One idea that was passed to Travis, when he was buying books, was to buy one and give one, that he thought would bring value to others in the same tone that it brought him. Opportunities began to open up to him and great things began to happen to him.

<u>The Benefit of the Benefit:</u> Do the positive things that successful people do and the benefits of doing so, will begin to unfold themselves to you. The additional benefits are that other people will notice the positive changes in your life. Doors will open to you that you didn't know existed. The blessings will come unto you. Be the person you are supposed to be and do the things you are supposed to do.

Chapter 2 – The Benefit of the Benefit

Have

Initially, we have talked about being the person you need to be. We further covered about doing the things you need to do; to continually be the person you are supposed to be. You will discover that you will begin to have positive things happen for you.

One of Zig Ziglar's most famous quotes is "You can have everything in life you want, if you will help enough people get what they want." You may be asking yourself, what does that have to do with me having what I want? It is about being a servant leader. As you begin to discover your why, I can tell you that at least a part of it will be serving others. Humans are social creatures and we are dependent on one another. A quote was revealed to Travis which was in alignment with his mindset and actions:

> *Work for a cause, not for applause.*
> *Live life to express, not to impress.*
> *Don't strive to make your presence noticed, strive to make your absence felt.*

I hope you understand that when you start making a positive impact on others, they will feel your absence when you are not around them. Success is not the limelight shining upon you, it is shining the light upon others. Celebrate others success around you. People will see your encouragement and they, in turn, will help you and celebrate with you on your successes. Travis learned this trait from his dad. His dad not only told him about the servant leader trait, he showed him by being a living example of serving others.

Chapter 2 – The Benefit of the Benefit

Travis, in turn, lived his life that way. I can guarantee you with 100 percent accuracy that is what he did. The twist to Travis' life is I am that adopted child. When my parents adopted me, they gave me my name. It wasn't until my early adulthood years that I learned my birth name. I firmly believe that if I had not been a servant leader to others, then the doors to get my adoption records unsealed would have never happened. I have been able to have the things in life that I have wanted ever since. I will continue to "Do" as I grow and develop. It is not a destination, it is a never-ending journey; a journey worth traveling since it only gets better as you grow, develop, and serve others. It all goes back to Zig's quote earlier of serving others.

<u>The Benefit of the Benefit</u>: You will be the person you are destined to be and will do the things you will need to do. The benefit will be having all that you want or desire. The greater benefit of the benefit is that you will be serving others to be, do, and have more. They, in turn, will be, do, and have more.

I am excited for you as you begin your journey of success and greatness. I recommend that you start today and work from the inside out. Be the person you are meant to be, and do the things you are supposed to do. Help others get what they want and you can have everything that you want. You have a choice in your life and I hope you make it a positive choice. The benefits will be great and the extended benefits will be even greater.

- Tracy D. Day

Chapter 2 – The Benefit of the Benefit

Chapter 2 – The Benefit of the Benefit

About the Author - Tracy D. Day

Tracy has worked in the information technology profession for nearly 30 years. As an infant, Tracy was adopted into a military household. Growing up in a military family and experiencing leadership throughout his young life, Tracy began his career in the United States Air Force and served nearly 14 years. He also owns a financial services business and is currently licensed at the state and federal levels.

Tracy was hand-selected by the Ziglar Corporation to be among the first 30 Ziglar Legacy Certified trainers and speakers in the world. He speaks on building winning relationships, goal setting and achievement, building a better you, and other leadership principles. In addition, he is a certified trainer in Human Behavior and Personality Traits.

Tracy is a life coach, motivational speaker, and a trainer. He has spoken for all types of organizations and is a key speaker for an international speaking organization.

Tracy is a contributing author in *Dare to Be A Difference Maker*, Volume 4 and Ziglar Legacy Books.

Being adopted into a loving family changed his life to the tune of having a good-natured, fun-loving attitude. He demonstrates that same attitude with his wife and three children. Tracy's approach and belief is to have a positive impact on everyone he meets and to make a difference in their life.

Email: Tracy@TracyDay.com

Chapter 2 – The Benefit of the Benefit

Chapter 3

Growth Has No Stop-Date
By Marie Calberry

The young baby yawned and stretched so hard it seemed that she would never stop. "That's how babies grow. She will never be as small again as she was before that big stretch," I said to my young daughter.
"Really?" was her surprised response. "Well, she will need good food, lots of giggles and cheers, and a family to teach and love her, but stretching is a huge part and necessary for her growth."

Years later both my daughter and I have experienced how true that is; not just for babies, and not just for physical growth, but in other areas and at all different ages. Life has ways of stretching us and teaching us about love, knowledge, wisdom, and gratitude. Sometimes it hurts so deeply you wonder if you will survive the stretch. Other times it seems only to be a minor diversion or interruption in our plans, yet at other times, life lessons are barely noticed, leaving us to wonder where we learned that concept. Regardless, we never come out on the other side the same.

My Dad loved to talk with people, and always had a joke or two ready. He could carry on a conversation with almost anyone.

Chapter 3 – Growth Has No Stop-Date

People would just drop into our yard and Dad was of course always happy to see them because a conversation was happening.

The conversational abilities of my Dad made it very inviting for me to follow him around chattering and asking questions. He never tired of responding to my childish inquiries. He would tell me family stories about how his Dad would love to laugh and play with the four children. His mother, however, would never allow laughter at the table, and how unsuccessful he was at turning off the giggles at mealtime, so he spent many meals sitting on the stairs. These times with my Dad were neither planned nor organized yet provided great classrooms of learning. I gained knowledge. I laughed. I felt important and loved, and I built a relationship with my Dad who, in my eyes, was ten feet tall. At the same time, my Dad was stretching and growing because growth has seasons, but no stop-date.

Over the course of my life, I have learned that there are several areas in which we need to stretch ourselves to keep growing. It is never enough to say that we have arrived. It is not healthy for us in either our personal lives or in our relationships with others to allow ourselves to stagnate and quit growing. Healthy relationships, healthy self-esteem and healthy personalities are based on continual, purposeful, intentional growth stretches in the areas of love, gratitude, knowledge, and wisdom.

So let's walk together through the next few pages and find out what I have learned and experienced in these areas.

Chapter 3 – Growth Has No Stop-Date

Grow in Love

Love is action, and with the action, there is a stretch. Love moves you to express that emotion. Even a cute puppy causes the hand of the viewer to reach out and touch him, and a smile to appear on the face. In response, the puppy's tail wags faster and his tongue connects with the hand that is petting him.

Sometimes the action of loving is wrapped up in taking time for the simple little things. Children may ask, "Watch me skate to the other side, Mom," or "Dad, did you see me catch that football?" or even the act of bringing someone coffee in bed, are all ways of stretching ourselves to show our love to someone.

My five-year-old great-grandson wanted to pet a squirrel. To be successful in his attempt he had to figure out how to get close enough without the squirrel scampering off. He thought that maybe if he used a nutcracker to crush up some nuts small enough to hide them in the bark of a tree that he might have a chance to actually pet a squirrel.

Alas, there were no nuts in the house, but there was a nutcracker. "Can we go to the store and buy some nuts, Dad?"

"Are you up to walking that far?" his father asked. So off they went, returning with great anticipation of enticing that squirrel to come close enough to be touched. The father assisted his son to strategically place the cracked nuts where the squirrel would certainly find them. Then the wait began. Waiting for the squirrel to show up quickly grew tiresome, and the watchers grew cold so they decided to wait in their car parked nearby. Soon the conversation in the car far outweighed the desire to pet a squirrel. You see, giving of your time is action and, therefore, giving of your time is love.

Chapter 3 – Growth Has No Stop-Date

In Zig Ziglar's words "To a child, love is spelled T.I.M.E." The father felt the last few hours had been worth the time and effort of trying to pet a squirrel.

Love demands action.
When a person truly loves, they are driven to show that love in real and tangible ways. It is the action of loving that causes one to undertake the often uncomfortable, stretching process. For example, some people are motivated to show their love by going into nursing homes and volunteering to sit with the frail or dying. This stretches them outside their comfort zone, yet they experience times of great satisfaction and even joy as they speak words of comfort and reassurance, pray with them, and just spend time with them. The giver realizes that the elderly do not feel abandoned or alone at this time of their life. The dying person may not respond, but they hear your words and feel your love as you sit by their bedside.

How about words of encouragement, instead of criticism, smiles instead of frowns, hugs instead of cold shoulders? There is no stop-date on cultivating these habits and allowing the aroma of love in action to escape, yet many of us need to be reminded often of these small expressions of love. Regardless how big or how small the action, love comes with a stretch at any age and by all kinds of people.

Jesus gives us the greatest example of love in action: "This is how we know what love is: Jesus Christ laid down His life for us. And we ought to lay down our lives for our brothers." 1 John 3:16 (NIV) The scriptures also tell us, "…let us not love with words or tongue, but with actions and in truth." 1 John 3:18 (NIV)

Chapter 3 – Growth Has No Stop-Date

The God of the Universe put love into action when He gave: "For God so loved the world that He gave His one and only Son, that whoever believes in Him shall not perish but have eternal life." John 3:16 (NIV)

Grow in Gratitude

Do you have a reason to be grateful today? That's OK. You don't need a reason. Gratitude is a choice.

There are days when being grateful is not something that happens easily. It occasionally takes perseverance and hard work. It requires a big stretch. Stop right now and think of one thing for which you are grateful…maybe it's life itself. Gratitude is not a behaviour modification; it's an attitude of choice.

Philippians 4:8 (NIV) says, "… if anything is excellent or praiseworthy — think about such things." As you choose to think about the positive and good things in life, your mind will develop an attitude of gratitude. For many of us, developing an attitude of gratitude is a huge stretch that can become life changing. Zig Ziglar said it best when he said, "Of all the attitudes we can acquire, the attitude of gratitude is the most important and by far the most life-changing."

Gratitude is stretching ourselves beyond looking at what is happening around us, and creating a thankful spirit for all things good, tangible and intangible. Everyone has something good in their life that they can be thankful for: love, family, friends, support, leaders, truth, excellence, etc. Sometimes it requires a little digging into ourselves to find that for which we can be thankful.

Chapter 3 – Growth Has No Stop-Date

Gratitude will shift the focus from the problem to the One who can change your outlook. It is during times of conflict and challenge when we need gratitude the most. When it doesn't feel good, when in the natural our situation looks bleak, and nothing seems to be going right, take out that pen and paper and write down at least one thing for which you are grateful, and then repeat it aloud several times. This brings two senses into agreement, the hearing and the seeing. Feeling will follow, but may have to be coaxed or coddled.

Gratitude must be intentional every day. We must keep it before us, in our minds and within view. That's where the pen and paper, or digital, become important tools of support. Ideas appear and disappear quickly, in and out of our thoughts, and need to be captured, jotted down, and made accessible when needed. Then, in our darkest times, we can read these statements of gratitude, and allow them to give wings to our spirit.

When I was growing up our family was never hungry nor cold, but we had no money. Our little farm supplied all our needs except cash. I wore hand-me-down clothes that were clean and neatly mended if necessary. These few articles of clothing were certainly not this year's designer pieces. I remember wearing a grey coat with large square buttons when I would go out to help with the chores.
I was fascinated with the buttons and remember touching them and thinking how "cool they were."
One evening I put my hand into the pocket and pulled out a piece of paper with these words printed on the front,

"Do You Know that Jesus Christ is Coming Back Again?"

Chapter 3 – Growth Has No Stop-Date

I felt like my heart was coming right up my throat as I tried to read the rest of the words. Now it was time to ask Dad about this. "Look what I found in my pocket, Dad. Is this true? What does it mean? When?"

It was probably the hardest question that I had ever asked him because you see he knew the way, but he was not walking therein at that time. I read and reread that piece of paper. It was not long following this that I became a believer, followed by my Dad, and shortly after by my Mother. Today I am still extremely grateful for the grey coat with the square buttons, with a message in the pocket. I am grateful that my Dad was honest with me even though it was difficult for him to admit he was not where he should be with God. I am filled with gratitude every time I think of all the clothing that was passed on to us, and for the person who put that tract in the pocket whether it was intentionally placed or not. Most of all, I am overflowing with gratitude for Jesus who made himself known to me in a very unconventional manner.

I like to think of gratitude as two-dimensional. Firstly, it reaches up to God. Our praise and thankfulness is to the One who loves us beyond words. Secondly, our gratitude reaches out to the people around us that mean so very much, from our closest family member to the clerk at the grocery checkout, or the person who drops cards and letters in our mailbox.

Let's have a 30-day stretch ... are you up for it? Write one or two items daily for which you are grateful. Don't repeat yourself. Make it something new every day.

It will be surprising to see how far you can come and how much you can grow in one month. Stretch big and make this activity intentional, a wise choice, and two-dimensional as you grow in gratitude.

Chapter 3 – Growth Has No Stop-Date

Grow in Knowledge and Wisdom

A boy went to his Dad and asked, "Dad, why does the wind blow?"

"I don't know," was the answer.

"Dad, why is the sky blue?"

"I don't know, son."

"Dad, do you mind me asking you these questions?" the boy asked.

"Oh, no son. How would you ever learn if you don't ask?"

Do you see what's missing here? Clearly there is a lack of knowledge as well as a lack of wisdom. Not everyone needs to know the answers to those particular questions. However, if the Dad had wisdom, but was lacking in knowledge, he could have said, "Let's find the answer together." Knowledge is easy to find today, but wisdom eludes us, maybe more so now than before access to information was available at our fingertips.

Knowledge and wisdom are a team. They must work together in unison.

Remember when you went to a country fair and watched the Belgian teams pulling the show carriage? Right feet up at the same time, necks curved with tightly braided manes, docked tails twitching, and traces tight and even as they proudly stepped around the ring almost as one animal. Knowledge and wisdom need that kind of maturity and practice to perform as a team.

Knowledge is needed. It feeds wisdom. Without knowledge, wisdom would be lacking and unable to make wise decisions, and give direction. "Wise people store up knowledge," Prov. 10:14 (NKJV)

Chapter 3 – Growth Has No Stop-Date

The way of least resistance is to "click" the remote, put your feet up, and be entertained by whatever the TV channels have prepared for you. Not a good habit for growth! Stretch! Pick up that book you've been intending to read and get started. Seek knowledge. "Apply your heart to instruction and your ears to words of knowledge." Proverbs 23:12 (NIV) Wisdom is the cruise control for knowledge. It sets boundaries and lines to guide us in our use of knowledge. When knowledge knows what to do, wisdom decides whether or not it should be done. "Wisdom is the principal thing; therefore get wisdom." Proverbs 4:7 (NKJV)

Develop wisdom.
When the Bible tells me in Proverbs 16:16 that it is better to get wisdom than gold, my mind is quickly made up. That is all the motivation I need to reach, stretch, and grow in wisdom throughout all stages of life. How do I do this? Again, the Bible has the answer in James 1:5 (NIV) "If any of you lacks wisdom, you should ask God, who gives generously to all without finding fault, and it will be given to you."

Wisdom is not talked about frequently, but it is often indirectly assumed. We may look at someone who has lived more years than we have, and assume that they are wiser. On the other hand, we may feel that because of all the social media and higher education around us today that this generation has more wisdom.

Neither years of life nor education can be credited for having wisdom in and of themselves. I believe that you can find knowledge in many places, but wisdom is developed with God's help. There is no stop-date on acquiring knowledge; and no stop-date on asking God for wisdom.

Chapter 3 – Growth Has No Stop-Date

The baby stretched again and yawned. "There she grows again!" my young daughter excitedly exclaimed. "If she keeps doing all that stretching, will she grow faster and become huge?" "I don't think she will become huge, but I do know that she will grow at a normal pace. All those stretches are good for her growth. And there will be many more stretches in her life before she is finished growing." I replied.

It is exactly the same for each one of us. Each time we stretch ourselves outside our comfort zone, we change; we grow. It may only be a little bit, but we grow. I know that as the years pass by, I can see the changes in myself that have taken place little by little, one stretch at a time. I can also clearly see that the stretches, the changes have not stopped. Every day I find God presents me with new challenges and situations that cause me to stretch and grow. It is a process that never stops. I believe that I will never be too old to stop growing and changing.

Now it's your turn; decision time. Will you choose to make some changes in your life by putting love into action, creating an attitude of gratitude, seeking knowledge, and becoming a wiser person?

Think of it this way, like a meditation:

"I am still stretching and growing like the little baby. My graduation day for growth has not arrived. The days that have passed on the calendar, few or many, do not give me a license to sit down and fold my hands, but rather to keep on reaching. Today this makes very little sense whatsoever. A year from now I'll wish I had started today."

Chapter 3 – Growth Has No Stop-Date

"We cannot start over, but we can begin now, and make a new ending." Zig Ziglar.

Today is the time to start. Actively seek new ways to stretch yourself beyond your comfort zone.

Look for simple ways to show your love to others. Begin today to intentionally and purposefully create a grateful lifestyle in yourself. Keep looking for opportunities to learn something new and expand your knowledge base. Apply what you learn to gain wisdom because there is no stop-date on improvement and growth.

- Marie Calberry

Chapter 3 – Growth Has No Stop-Date

Chapter 3 – Growth Has No Stop-Date

About the Author - Marie Calberry

Marie has been a teacher, a church and community leader, a registered nurse, owner of a small business, and an entrepreneur. In addition, she currently serves as vice chair on the Board of Directors of a not-for-profit company.

Marie is a Ziglar Legacy Certified Trainer and Speaker offering encouragement to others to be the best they can be, motivation to set and achieve goals and the need to learn to celebrate individual and group successes.

Marie has four successful and supportive grown children. When they were growing up, winter weekends were spent on the ski hills where Marie was a member of the ski patrol. She remains passionate about sports and believes many life lessons are learned on the hills, in the rink, or on the football field.

You may contact Marie at mariecalberry@gmail.com
Like her on Facebook
Follow her on Twitter Anne Calberry @ACalberry

Chapter 3 – Growth Has No Stop-Date

Chapter 4

A Working Definition
By Mindy Turner

One day my youngest son, then five years old, was telling me what he wanted to be when he grows up. As with any child, this is an ongoing discussion. On this particular day, he was talking about being a doctor. We talked about helping people when they are sick or hurt. Knowing how much he loves animals, I explained that a veterinarian was a doctor for animals. He took it all in. Big eyes trusting me for all the answers, as he asked those important questions that would help determine his future goals – at least for the next couple of hours. Finally, with a serious nod, he said, "Ok Mommy, I will be a doctor, but can I still be Batman?" Without missing a beat, I replied, "Yes, you can be Batman."

We have all heard it said that everyone has a defining moment. In that moment, my son defined himself as Batman (a mother could do worse). The key to keeping a positive mindset is to understand that it is not "a" defining moment, but rather defining moments: plural. You will have many throughout your lifetime. Even better, the one who writes the definition is you. While your goals may not be so lofty as to be Batman, you define those goals. You choose your moments.

Chapter 4 – A Working Definition

When my oldest son was six, he was having a tough time at daycare. Through a series of conversations and subtle questions (by the way, subtle questions are not really the way to go with a six-year-old), we discovered that he was upset because in racing with the older boys on the playground, he couldn't win. While we don't focus on winning, he has a natural understanding of competition. This was an excellent opportunity for us as parents to talk about the value of focusing on doing your best, setting a goal and working toward it, to not be defined by a race.

My husband, a wise man in more ways than just his choice of bride, is a horse guy. Knowing that my son also loves horses and has seen *Secretariat* too many times to count, he brought home some history about Secretariat and Seabiscuit, both famous racehorses. Most people don't realize that these famous horses lost more races than they won, particularly in the beginning. Succeeding at anything takes time, effort and focus.

With this in mind, my son began to practice. He ran all the time, begging us to race him at every opportunity. While he didn't win every race, he did manage to win a few. Fast forward two years later and he won every event at his 1st grade field day, even running anchor for his class relay team. I wouldn't be surprised if he continues with track when he is older. He is not a track star, he is seven. He is not defined by winning or losing a race, but by setting a goal and working toward it. This has helped him succeed in his school work, at horse shows and in other activities. He has learned to choose what matters, learned from failure and focus on his vision.

Chapter 4 – A Working Definition

Growing up, I was blessed to have all of my grandparents in my life. We were all right there in the same town. I was in and out of their houses as much as my own. My love of reading, crafting and baking all come from my grandmothers and their tutelage when I was a child.

Great aunts and uncles, a slew of cousins extended family galore. When you grow up in this environment, it never occurs to you that there will be a time in your life when these people are not there. A friend once told me you can expect to lose your parents and grandparents in your lifetime. While technically that is true, none of us ever really expect it. In particular, we don't expect to lose them before they ever pass away.

Within the past two years, my maternal grandmother, whom I grew up right down the road from, was diagnosed with dementia. Dementia is one of those things that sneaks up on you, but once someone whispers the word, you can reflect back on a hundred little signs that were there all along. All those little moments we chalk up to old age or stress and write off as just the way things are, never giving them the credit they deserve, until one day they are so prevalent or so colossal, you have to come face-to-face with the situation. The reality of DEMENTIA…there is no way to stop it or bypass it.

By the time it has a name, by the time you know it is what it is, the progression seems accelerated. Whether it really is, or it is just that now you are hyper-sensitive to the signs, is hard to say. It is hard on the one with dementia, and hard on the family.

Chapter 4 – A Working Definition

With my grandmother, she went from telling me on the phone to get on my tricycle and come down to her house, seeing me as a little girl, to her believing I was my mother at this age. Finally, she began to think of me as her sister (one or the other) at my age, which would have been thirty-forty years ago. To where we are today – she sees a kind person that comes to see her, but no recollection of who I am or how she might know me.

The heartbreak of dementia is seeing her frustration as she knew what was happening; she knew what she didn't know. She knew she couldn't find her words and things came out wrong. She knew she should be able to complete simple tasks, but couldn't figure out how. My brother summed it up when he said: "You would think they could just forget everything and be happy all the time." We wanted that for her – instead, it was a daily heartbreak. Not knowing who is with you or where you are, not knowing who has passed away – never knowing when it would hit.

The Notebook is a bestselling novel written by Nicholas Sparks. It was made into a blockbuster movie, still referenced in current shows and literature, even after more than ten years. I read the book and loved it. As a matter of fact, my second date with my husband was to see *The Notebook* at the movies. It is an emotional and powerful story of a young couple. How they met, fell in love and overcame obstacles to be together. It is about love and loyalty and family – it is about commitment. Most of the story is told in flashback as you get to know the couple, now elderly, living in a nursing home and the wife has dementia.

Chapter 4 – A Working Definition

In one part, the couple's children are telling Noah (their father and the husband of the dementia patient) he should move home, rather than staying with his beloved wife in the nursing home. They say to him "She doesn't even know who you are." His response is, and this is epic, "What difference does that make? I know who she is."

When I look at my grandmother, all I can think is, "What a blessing that I know who she is." She was an anchor in our lives. Married at fifteen, raising three children, going on to get her GED, in the workforce when necessary, in the home when necessary. Caring for her aging parents, aunts, siblings…and for her young grandchildren. She never complained and she never judged. It was common to hear her say "That's them for it," whenever one of us might express disagreement with someone else's behavior.

I have one of her Bibles – it is worn with a broken spine and well-worn pages, a testimony to her faithfulness. She kept journals when she and my grandfather travelled, a testimony to her appreciation for the opportunities she was given. I have her Christmas tree (don't tell my cousins), the one that stood in her house every year throughout my childhood (yes, it is older than I am) and this year I cried as I put it up in my home to share it with my own children – who I am thankful every day got to know her.

These are the things that define her, these moments and memories. Not a broken hip and a diagnosis of dementia, but 70 years of marriage and loyalty to the same man, who will still tell you they are on "speaking and kissing terms." He speaks to her and she tells him to kiss her foot. Laughter and love…a legacy.

Chapter 4 – A Working Definition

The pastor put it so beautifully in a sermon about Moses. So close to what is in my heart. Legacy is what you leave behind. Sometimes we don't get to finish the journey we begin. But we can leave a legacy behind so that others may finish. Moses served God until the end, even when he didn't get to enter the Promised Land. Legacy means you do your part, whatever your part may be. Do what God asks you to do and that is enough. You may not win every race – you may not get to be Batman, but you move the master plan forward. You have a purpose.

We all have failures – we allow ourselves to get caught up in a moment – to stunt our own growth by putting a negative definition on that moment and beating ourselves up over it. Moses failed, he did not get to lead his people into the Promised Land. He did not let his failure keep him from serving the Lord, he accepted his consequences and left behind his legacy. For many of us the idea of "unfinished" is hard to accept. I will be honest, I am that person who adds a task I have already completed, that wasn't on the list, to the list so I can check it off. My least favorite chore is laundry, not because it is hard, but because it is never really "finished" unless your entire family is naked! It is hard for me to accept that I will never really be "finished." And then I see my grandmother, whom I am learning from even today, and I look at my children who I am also learning from.

If she could articulate it, I am sure my grandmother would say she is not "finished," but she doesn't have to be. She can be at peace with where she is, who she is because she leaves behind a legacy for others to build on. One of strength and integrity. Investing in people builds a legacy. She invested daily in this family.

Chapter 4 – A Working Definition

She is one of the valuable influences that allows me to invest in my family, my career and my own legacy daily.

I hope to have the opportunity at some point to write about all of my grandparents. They were/are amazing. Though they would tell you they were ordinary people, just living the best they could. They inspire me, more importantly, knowing them helps define me. I am well aware that everyone doesn't have close family. They may not have had the opportunity to know them, or may be estranged from them in some way. But, there are people in your life every day who can and will inspire you. Some over long periods of time, some in a moment.

Some may be characters in a book or movie, an author reaches you through them. Someone you never met, but saw a video online or quote shared on social media. It speaks to you. Reminds you to consider your moments and define them as only you can do. A teacher, a friend, that person you met on the plane or the bus and had a brief conversation with. They influence you. You become part of their legacy.

I was on my way home from a conference and was seated next to an elderly gentleman on the plane. This had to be twelve years ago, but I remember him vividly. His name was Floyd and he was wonderful. We got started talking and he was on his way home from visiting one of his grown children. His wife had passed away just a year ago. About the same time, I lost my paternal grandmother. He had lost a son in a motorcycle accident – I had recently had an uncle killed on his motorcycle. The timing was all God. I know that. Floyd allowed me to revisit those moments of loss and

Chapter 4 – A Working Definition

redefine them as stopping points in a life that was continuing on. It was an hour flight – it was a lifetime of insight. You never know when you will be someone's Floyd or who that person will be for you.

You see, those defining moments are what we call a "working definition." Time and perspective change and grow them. The definition is never truly finished, it is ongoing.

For every person that influences you, you influence someone else. It doesn't have to be in a big, earth-shattering, lightning strike. It is in moments. You inspire others and they become part of your legacy.

I recently did a workshop for seventy-five teenagers on building relationships. Trust me, every time I teach, I think I learn more from the participants than they do from me. That is probably why I love it. At the end of the program, I asked them to write down something that spoke to them; a quote, an attitude change, or an ah-ha moment. One youth wrote: "I have an impact on people and I don't realize it. I can impact more lives than I think I can." When I saw this note on a torn off piece of paper not even a quarter of a sheet – I thought, this kid gets it. It is so easy to become caught up in the daily struggle – whether it's drudgery, like doing laundry, or the heartbreak of physical and mental illness in those we love – we are impacting, we are building a legacy, we are defining.

My six-year-old recently broke his arm, again. Yes, again, the same arm. I kept saying it was the same place. My brother finally said, "I bet it is not the same place, they usually knit

Chapter 4 – A Working Definition

together stronger after they have been broken." It hurts a little when he is right – gut reaction of a younger sister, but in this case, he was correct. When a broken bone heals, the place where the break was is now the strongest part of that bone. It is in the moments we are broken that we find true strength, that we find definition, that we find purpose.

My life is made up of moments. Some feel good, some feel uncomfortable, and let's face it, some feel bad – but all are teaching, all are growing, all are mine. They are not finished, they are ongoing and they build strength. They do not define me, I define them. They make me part of a legacy, they allow me to create a legacy. Embrace these moments. They will never come again in quite the same way. Embrace the people who create them, for better or worse, sometimes your biggest challenge becomes your biggest strength.

I don't know your story, but I would love to hear it. Within the chapter of a book, I can only share a handful of moments. Thank you for taking the time to become part of my legacy. Now, go forward and make someone a part of yours. Be ongoing.

- Mindy Turner

Chapter 4 – A Working Definition

Chapter 4 – A Working Definition

About the Author – Mindy Turner

Mindy Turner is no stranger to negativity and personal challenges, but with positive thinking, all things are possible.

Zig Ziglar tells us "You are who you are and what you are because of what has gone into your mind. You can change who you are and what you are by changing what goes into your mind." Let Mindy Turner help you identify the positive influences in your life and how you can be a positive influence in the lives of others.

Offering hands-on, interactive workshops, Mindy has successfully helped youth and adults strengthen relationships, set achievable goals and become the leaders they were meant to be! With over 20 years of experience in youth organizations, and now as a Ziglar Legacy Certified Trainer, Mindy can meet you where you are and introduce you to where you are going! Join us and begin your journey to Building the Best You!

Mindy can be contacted via email at teamsense.turner@gmail.com or through Facebook at www.Facebook.com/TeamSenseMindyTurner

Chapter 4 – A Working Definition

Chapter 5

The Warrior Who Painted Her Fight
By Manu Shahi

My story is one that you have probably read before. I am not the only one who has been through this. After me, unfortunately, more will continue to walk this path. The past is a just in my memory, the future is my imagination, but the present is the only reality. Once I learned how to accept this fact, I end my suffering. The more we dwell on the *what's* and *whys* of life, the deeper we will get attached to the past. If we make plans about what is yet to come, our imagination will have no limit. This is something we all know, but only the experiences of life, and how we handle the journey time and time again, help us to implement it into our own lives.

It was 2004, on a cold winter Tuesday evening around 7:45 pm. The table was set with candles, a bottle of champagne and light music. There was a small princess cake for three; it was a date with destiny. A date that had been marked on the calendar two and half years in advance for Jan. 13, 2004. Hallucinatory by nature, planning and looking forward to special moments before they occurred was part of my basic nature. They say the more we plan, the deeper the expressions of joy or pain will be when the event happens.

Chapter 5 – The Warrior Who Painted Her Fight

Perhaps my date was not planned well enough, for I hope it does not take a lifetime for me to take it one step at a time. On the menu we had fresh, home cooked food that comprised of sautéed eggplant, black lentil with kidney beans and fresh homemade bread. How much food can an almost 5-year-old eat? Being a mother and an investor by profession, at that time, I knew that devoting good food would create a happy tummy for our young daughter. A happy tummy leads to good times later in life, or at least in our case, hours for sure.

Even though it had been a very long day, the journey to get to this date had been longer. Eager to celebrate the end of a victorious passage in life, I asked my husband to take the champagne out of the refrigerator for us to toast. The day required nothing less than to mark the moment. He had forgotten to set the champagne on the table as he was too busy playing Lego's with our daughter. In an attempt to get up and grab the bottle, I realized the home phone was also not on the table. As a family, we had a habit of keeping the phone near us when we had dinner. We did this just in case it rang, as our family who lives overseas called. They always called during this time to check on our daughter to see how her day was going. I attempted to push the chair back to get up, grab the phone and the bottle, as I wanted the moment to be perfect. Considering the distance from the table to the fridge, to celebrate today, I never knew would take another three years for me to travel.

As soon as I got up, the phone rang, but this ring echoed for a lifetime.

Chapter 5 – The Warrior Who Painted Her Fight

It started another chapter without letting the first one complete. The caller ID read it was the Oncologist from Children's Hospital. Answering the phone with excitement and gratitude, I greeted her oncologist. I started to thank him for everything he had done for us in the last 2 ½ years. I told him we were about to start dinner, but I could tell something was different in his voice. As he spoke, the words seemed to be bouncing back to me after it felt like they were hitting the wall. His verses were echoing to me. His silence on the other side made me wonder why a doctor would call so late on a Tuesday. Usually, the processing speed of my brain would let me jump ahead and figure out the *what's* and *whys*, but this time, with the bottle and the cake, the anticipated moment had arrived and this phone call was stopping me from living it.

"Mrs. Shahi, I am afraid I have some bad news for you about your daughter." That was his opening line. That sentence just took me back to what had happened 2 ½ years prior. My mind replayed the moment and that sentence sounded so very familiar. Of course, it had been said to me before. Was history repeating itself or was I drunk without the champagne? Was the earth frozen or was I going back in time due to excitement? Confused or excited, like the Texas weather that I lived with for the last 10 years, I definitely was not sure what part of "I have bad news" I was dealing with. Previously, on July 13th, 2001, there was a deviation in my journey of life that I had accepted without questioning any higher power. I had worked towards saving my then 2 ½-year-old daughter from fighting leukemia. It was a firm decision made without any second thoughts.

Chapter 5 – The Warrior Who Painted Her Fight

In life, they say losing your parents makes you feel very lonely. It doesn't matter how big your family is or how old they are. It feels as if the roots are gone and the survival skills they taught are being put to good use. In comparison, I can assure you the thought of losing a child makes you feel as if someone just punched your gut, took out your heart and placed it in your palm and said, it will stop beating soon. In 2001, as a mother, the only words I said to the doctors were, "You do what you have to do and I will make sure it goes the right way for you and is comfortable for her. You do your job and I will do mine." At that moment, I had decided to accept the present without anyone preaching or being given numerous self-help books or even searching for spiritual guidance. They were not required, as for now, living in the moment was the best choice.

We all have these characteristics that are talked about, claim, or that others see, but we personally don't see it. It is only during hardship that the real personality comes out of a human soul. How we panic, handle the circumstances, the emotions and how we get up from getting knocked down is what defines us at that moment. However, no one needs to define anyone, as life does a great job on its own. Just like today was the end of her treatment and now life was supposed to get back on track. She was supposed to have a normal life, start Kindergarten in the fall and attend birthday parties. She was supposed to go to theme parks and use all of the hair accessories that were in a big bag that had been collected over time by a desperate mother. The anticipation of this day, where we could go back to who we were, was such a false hope that was given by no one else but ourselves.

Chapter 5 – The Warrior Who Painted Her Fight

The reality is that we had no idea where life was taking us, but it surely could never go back to where it was. It happened for a reason. We just didn't know why. It created an insecurity as the moment made us unsure about anything going forward.

As her parents, we made the best of those times and years. We spent numerous hours and days in the hospital, but we made sure life looked normal for her. No, I am not claiming that we did anything that special. But even though the pain was exhausting for her and seeing her in soreness was heartbreaking, we pretended that this was a normal lifestyle since she had no one to compare with at that age. It was the three of us against Dragon Boo-Boo. That was the name she called this uninvited guest that had to be shooed away by Simba, as she proudly addressed herself.

Did I forget to read the rules from the game book of Life? The part where they tell you to only see as far as you can see and once you reach that point to dream further; but to not stress out if you cannot see the end. However, the team of professionals had shown us the end. They told us this chapter would end in 2 ½ years. How could we forget to read the fine print? It clearly said that 95% of the patients do fine. I never knew that she was in the top five percent of the special kids that are supposed to learn lessons early on in life. The 2 ½ years went by so fast with hospital stays, treatment plans, and accepting the new normal. The new life never gave me permission to sense what was going on and do what normal people do, like indulge in the self-pity "Why Me" drill. I'm not sure if time had allowed this thought to turn

Chapter 5 – The Warrior Who Painted Her Fight

into actions and then into the words to enter my mind, but the final destination was so clear; it really did not matter.

While the doctor was still talking on the phone, the 2 ½ years came back to me in just two seconds. It was January and a thin layer of ice had started to form outside the house and also inside of me. It happened as the doctor told me that my little girl's cancer was coming back in a more aggressive form. They didn't know how and why it relapsed, but it was more resilient than before. After a certain point in the conversation, his voice seemed like noise, not words and was not making sense. I just wanted to hang up, but my hand, like my heart, was now numb. He asked me to come into the office to meet with him and talk about it. I was not sure what to ask, how to react or how to respond. I listened to everything he said. What just happened? The ice from outside, once again uninvited, seemed to enter my house making every single cell in my body cold. It seemed to reach my brain just as it decided to shut down. My heart was beating so loud that I felt like looking for earmuffs to warm it up. However, my soul was still alive.

She was reading my expressions and I didn't want her to feel anything that was remotely painful. Not today. Even though the uninvited guest that arrived on July 13th, 2001 decided to stay with us just a little longer, today was not the day I wanted to entertain him. I picked up my daughter after she was done with her dinner and went inside her room. With my warm soul and frozen body, I hugged her tight. I read her the Lion King book so that this little warrior could sleep to fight another battle.

Chapter 5 – The Warrior Who Painted Her Fight

That night everything appeared like a noisy possession that kept passing in the front of our house. No matter how many doors and windows were being shut down, it still echoed and entered the house to a mother's heart.

Quite often we start doing things that we are told we're good at. Very rarely we give up on things that we are told we're bad at because the ego plays an interfering role. On several turns of our journey, I was told by people that I had courage and strength to deal with life. I have always felt that this is true for all of us. A special someone once said that I had the Midas touch. However, I strongly believe that anything done with sincerity and purity turns into gold. When we least expect it, life gives us a challenge to test our courage and willingness to change.

Was I planning to take life for granted again? Maybe I had not learned the lesson yet. Perhaps something bigger was on the horizon. I felt that at such a moment, there was no point in pretending that nothing had happened because I knew the challenge would not wait. Life does not look back. Once we face it and live in the moment by accepting it, nothing could stop us from moving forward again. This was something that I knew I was born with, as it is my elementary nature. My parents had nurtured me to be independent and strong, perhaps for this.

In 2001, the first time when we got the news, I was alone in the hospital as my husband had to run to the immigration office. We had taken the oath as U.S. citizens that week, but the INS office had to correct the name on the paperwork. The pediatrician had sent us to the ER for her leg pain which

Chapter 5 – The Warrior Who Painted Her Fight

she assumed was a hairline fracture. Neither one of us knew what kind of medical journey was marching forward.

That fracture would actually break every single bone in our bodies, damage our nerves and attempt to kill our souls as we confirmed the real news of her diagnosis. In 2004, this was unexpected too. Perhaps big things happen when we least expect them. That was an evening of my life.

After helping my daughter fall fast asleep, it was time to talk as a couple to see what exactly had happened. I walked into the family room, where my husband was sitting down looking outside into a dark night. I saw he had wrapped up the untouched dinner and picked up the plates, as we had lost our appetites. What should I tell him? How do the words I can't believe, get translated? It was just a moment that came and went away, right? I wanted to hug him, but he wanted to talk. This time, as a couple we had a difference on how we were responding to the news. This time, for my husband, his princess was trapped by the dragon again and he so wanted to save her. Perhaps this is one of the hardest things for a father. I could see history repeating where he as a man, was going into a shell. His shell was very strong and the pearl inside him, his heart, seemed to be melting and he could not express himself. That might be a gender thing where silence speaks to men and for women, words make us quiet. As my husband and her father, I knew it had to be a challenge to see his kingdom being invaded by the same dragon twice.

We discussed the few options that the doctor had mentioned over the phone. The issue could be just a viral infection she was fighting, but seemed questionable, or it could be a

Chapter 5 – The Warrior Who Painted Her Fight

recurrence of her cancer or something that they did not know at that point. Optimistic by nature, he was swayed that this was a viral infection that she was fighting and that she would recover on her own. Practical by nature, though emotional, I was swayed to the other side.

He took the least common method and I took the highest common the doctor gave. His optimism made him comfortable in his precinct. On the other hand, as a mother, I was not sure what I was feeling. I wanted to enter his precinct, but I could not. They say a mother's gut feeling is very strong, but I hated my instinct that day. It was best that my heart was frozen, for if it had melted, the salty ocean from my heart to my eyes would have melted everyone. It was not just about the three of us. It touched her grandparents, who were living overseas. They only had hope and imagination to live by on by what and how we worded the events to them. There is a tendency at every important, but difficult crossroad to pretend that it's not really there. He was pretending and I wanted to pretend. How could we solve the problem until we both acknowledged that we had one? We could only move forward once we accepted the responsibility to solve it.

The next day was an early cold winter morning. I had to get ready to meet the team of doctors at the hospital. The team consisting of an oncologist, a pathologist and senior doctor who all wanted to discuss the new treatment plan. One of the strengths of our marriage has always been that during a crisis we have this silent understanding; who will be the caregiver and who takes the role of the breadwinner.

Chapter 5 – The Warrior Who Painted Her Fight

We both knew each other's strengths and weaknesses. One thing we worked well on was research and educating ourselves.

As I was getting ready to head to the hospital, I was handed a list of questions ready to ask the team. They wanted to meet up to explain what was going on with my little warrior, who was now four weeks away from turning five.

Before entering the arena again, or I should say I never got a chance to exit, I was face down one more time in life. As I drove out of my driveway to start round two of this battle, the little girl in me wanted to run to my father and hide as if this was just a nightmare. The little girl in me wanted to hold his hand, ask him a zillion questions and feel his hand on my head. I closed my eyes as I sat in the car. I could feel my mom's hand on my head like she always did when I went for my exams. I could feel my dad cupping my face in his palms, kissing my forehead and saying, "There is no such thing as difficulty in life, only great challenges which ordinary people rise to meet. You are born to be a warrior. I have asked you from God in my prayers. You are special. Remember that: You can do it."

Nothing is predestined. The obstacles and experiences from my past became the gateways that led to new beginnings. I knew this place. I identified the terminology the doctors used. I knew the floor I was walking on. Entering the oncology unit reminded me once again of the time 2 ½ years back when I had crossed the threshold through the ER. History and future were fighting a battle in my head while I was focusing on the present.

Chapter 5 – The Warrior Who Painted Her Fight

What am I supposed to do, again? What does this entail for me and my family? Will I be able to handle it or will I fail? All of these unanswered questions felt like another layer of ice on me and I felt numb. That was good because I had no room for pain at this time, but a small candle was burning inside of me and I called it hope. It was a torch that was protected by faith and my belief that nothing can go wrong because positive thinking leads to a life full of color and experience.

Suddenly, the elevator door opened to little kids running around the floor. They were cheerful to get a sticker for being poked or a toy for getting a spinal tap. Some had tears for fear of seeing the doctor or the child life specialist, who do play therapy with a sick child. As the receptionist called my name, a few of the nurses looked at me with pity and some with courage. Some had tears in their eyes while some just held my hand. Soon, I was told to take a seat in the meeting room. This time it was not the procedure room, the playroom for patients or the recovery room. It was the cold (like my body temperature) conference room.

The doctors said, "We have not seen anything like this before. She was doing well and we could have never anticipated this coming. At this point, we don't know what to say, but we can figure out a plan for her. We can wait, not that we would recommend that, but it needs to be treated for sure and further testing needs to be done. It is coming back as cancer, but a different kind and way more hostile than the first time. Typically, the treatment for this type is a bone marrow transplant. But since you are of South-Asian origin,

Chapter 5 – The Warrior Who Painted Her Fight

it is hard to find a match. So doing an unrelated cord blood transplant is perhaps the best option. It can be done here at this hospital. We have a small section that is dedicated to BMT patients. They stay in isolation for 100 days at the hospital and one year indoors. The survival rate at this point is very low, around 20%. We are sorry." And they were done. They finished as if I was just another file that they were talking about. Maybe they were numb just like me.

I sat in the room writing my meeting notes. I was soaked in tears, filled with fear and I hated every word they said. I wanted to cry; to melt. I wanted to go on my knees and ask Him only one question: "When I accepted it gracefully the first time, why are you doing this again?"

Once again, I pushed the chair to get up, but before I left the hospital, this is what the mother in me declared to them: "She is my daughter, my only daughter and I will save her…no matter what. Thank you for your time. I will get back with you."

That was the start of my new journey.

I arrived home and my husband, who was taking care of her opened the door for me. How would I tell him what they just told me about the treatment? I knew deep inside that he had been doing research online during his long nights of studying. I was so wrapped up in fixing my own mind and bandaging my own pain that I realized even though holding hands or rubbing my back was comforting, it was also making me weak. The warmth would melt the ice and that wouldn't be good. I needed to gain strength, energy and get moving as time was not on my side again.

Chapter 5 – The Warrior Who Painted Her Fight

Someone once told me that emotional pain is only 20 minutes long, the rest of the pain is self-inflicting. Even though the pain I was hiding was 30 months long, it was time to freeze it again.

We discussed the treatment plan, the pre-treatment journey, and life, but we never gathered the courage to discuss the "What about the 20% chance?" question, as if it wasn't a possibility. My faith and his confidence never let us cross that line of conversation. Moreover, we knew our world would just crumble if that occurred. We were determined to give her the best treatment plan that this country had to offer. Don't they say that America is the land of opportunity and where dreams come true? Keeping in mind that she needed an unrelated cord blood transplant, we decided to pack up and move temporarily to North Carolina to get her treatment at Duke Hospital.

Our research and the conversations with the medical team made us feel at ease. We were also able to find a match for her in a matter of one week. We knew the game plan, but we were definitely not ready for the game yet. Our Bodies, minds, and souls had to be prepared. One thing we found out was that the doctor we were talking to, had gifted hands and an amazing soul. He was a doctor that was as calm as the sea and was hopeful like a ray of sunshine after the storm. Without even visiting the hospital, I knew this was the answer. He comforted us by saying we could wait and take the time to get over our fears as long as her blast (cancer cells) were under a certain percentage. He was always on call with a tone that comforted us like Zoloft.

Chapter 5 – The Warrior Who Painted Her Fight

I saw it as a blessing that my child was small enough to not understand this language. All she wanted was mom and dad next to her and playtime with her few close friends. She was amazing and funny with the nurses. Every doctor just adored this little girl whose hugs made them fall in love with her. All I had to tell this warrior was that Dragon Boo-Boo was back and that we were ready for the war to begin. She was called my warrior. I prepared her mind by telling her that she is a soldier and her body by drinking wheat grass juice every day. If anyone has tasted that juice, you know what I'm talking about. She was getting ready to fight this dragon. She would drink that juice pretending that it was a magic potion that Dragon Boo-Boo was afraid of. With every finger poke she pretended she was Sleeping Beauty and every time she had fish she pretended she was a mermaid. Her imagination was like a rainbow; we knew where it would end and we would get a pot of gold filled with smiles and laughter at the end. That was the image and the positive thinking we all had deep in our hearts. We knew the worst, but we imagined and attracted the best.

The fretfulness, dread and restlessness started to kick in as the silence of time started. Every blood work would mess with my anxiety level making me nervous and panicky. Even with all the noise of the children's hospital, the moment the nurse walked out of the lab with her results and counts, I could hear her footsteps getting louder as she approached with the marks. As she started talking I could still hear her footsteps echoing in my ear. She repeated: "Mrs. Shahi, we have the results for your daughter." Without saying a word, she would go over all her counts, but my ears now were just

Chapter 5 – The Warrior Who Painted Her Fight

waiting for two words only "Blast Cells." I had mixed feeling this time. My outer shell was all ready to take the challenge, but my inner-self was questioning my own strength. Asking myself: Was I ready again? What if? And how long? These questions kept me up at night while I held her hand and rubbed her back to make her fall asleep. I knew I had to take care of my physical health to take care of my inner soul. They say a lot of caretakers are so into taking care of the patient that they forget they exist too, me included. But this time, I had the awareness of how intense the journey would be and my mind and body had to be prepared. I was not being selfish, but I was more like the commander-in-chief of the army, getting ready to direct the war. First the soul, then the body.

I tried meeting up with a physiologist to discuss the fears I had, but after a session or two, it made me realize, not right now. Through all of this, I came across a book that practically held on to me for years called *"Where There is Light"* by Paramahansa Yogananda. It answered my questions and gave me the support I needed at that point. What worked for me might not work for others, but the very nature of not giving up was my strength and the gamble I was ready to take. Once again, I wanted to deal with the present, not dwell on the past or bother myself with questions that I wanted someone to answer. I would not give up on my daughter. That's all.

While we were in the waiting period, a turning point happened in our life. It was a point that changed her life and others and impacted us forever.

Chapter 5 – The Warrior Who Painted Her Fight

One day, while in the hospital, waiting for her doctor, she asked me about Make-A-Wish Foundation (they grant wishes for kids with life-threatening medical conditions). She asked if they would grant another wish for her since she was diagnosed again. It was a valid question from a 5-year-old who had ended up going on a magic carpet with Aladdin and Jasmine. She had hugged the Beast in front of the Beauty and sung her favorite song with Simba himself at the *"Lion King"* show. Unfortunately, they only grant wishes once in a lifetime. At that moment, my princess was coloring in her book and was doing such an amazing job with her color sense. I looked into her eyes and said, "Let's change the rules princess. It's time for *us* to grant wishes. Let's paint so that this world can see how beautiful this earth is from your eyes only."

The team at Make-A-Wish Foundation had been very supportive even after the fact that her wish had already been granted. As a mother, my idea was to have her be in touch with those who were in a similar boat, through formal and informal connections (those who made her feel comfortable) so that she would not feel alone undergoing this kind of treatment. The magic moment happened with us right there when she popped that question and my answer helped add a little cushion to her journey she was about to undertake. I told her that while they are doing the fighting, we should paint the world to be a better and brighter place. With that paint, we will grant wishes instead. It was a promise made by a mom, but I had no idea how I was going to execute it. Something about moms; they can see without eyes, smell without noses and feel without a touch.

Chapter 5 – The Warrior Who Painted Her Fight

No matter what, she was a part of me. I saw her coloring and I knew she could make a difference.

The faith and trust a 5-year-old has in a mother is unbelievable. You love, yet you are afraid and you never want to break that trust. This is especially true when she asks with her innocent look and twinkle in her eyes, "Is everything going to be okay mom? Is Dragon Boo-Boo going to die? Simba still has to fight Uncle Scar right?" There were so many questions to be answered by someone who did not have any answers, but who had her. There is a thin line between hope and denial, and that line is a firm commitment to truth and reality.

False hope can lead to unbalanced choices and imperfect decision making. True hope takes into account the real fears that exist and pursues the best path to take. My hope was the practical and best possible way to handle the treatment. The other half was being optimistic that we could make it happen. His love, my determination and the wishes from people all around the world took us to this next phase of our journey. We lived every day as if it was the first day of our life not the last. Looking back was not an option, but finding the solution to what we had in our hands was the only thing in my mind. Perhaps that was maybe the only moment when I lived in the present.

As the weather changed, I had hoped it would change my destiny too. Days were longer, birds were chirping and a ray of hope was entering inside that this would go away. I wanted my husband to win with the fact that it was just a virus. My mother, who I had called, from India, spent endless hours

Chapter 5 – The Warrior Who Painted Her Fight

praying and sending good vibrations in the house. Her silence and praying made me weak. I knew her hope was going up, but so were my daughter's cancer cells. Her clinic day was on a Tuesday and I waited outside in the patient waiting room for the results. I could feel my heart inside of my throat. Books, meditation centers, yoga and all forms of healing were presented to me. I knew the power and answers to train my brain was within me. When I read the book *"The Dance of Connection,"* by Harriet Lerner, I learned that we all have a patterned way of managing stress and anxiety. I was for sure the over-functioning type, not the under-functioning. I was always ready to advise, rescue, take over, micromanage and basically get into other people's business at times. The blast cells were up and it was time to head north.

It was on my birthday that the final telephone call came from the hospital that her cells were getting high and a transplant would need to happen. It was Father's day, 2004, when we packed up our bags and took a flight to start the next chapter of our life. In between that time, we took care of things like wrapping up the house, following step-by-step instructions on how to pack our bags for the hospital, what kind of clothes she could wear, how to keep her busy and more. Once again, the emotional silence and the mental stress was much louder than my heartbeat. It was time for the flight to take off and start the new journey where everything would change forever. It could go either way. Relationships, experiences, tolerance and even the blood; all would have new meaning and new limits for us. As I was about to enter the plane, I held my husband's hand looking for

Chapter 5 – The Warrior Who Painted Her Fight

confirmation that we did all that we could as parents and now it is destiny. Wishing is the fantasy that everything is going to turn out OK. Hoping is actually showing up for the hard work. We showed up at the hospital to get started. What an army of three soldiers we were!

Before the first night at the new apartment, we stayed at the Courtyard Inn by Marriott. To make her comfortable (and ourselves physically too), we rented furniture for the next few months. We took a few trips to Walmart to buy basic household needs. We accustomed ourselves to the new roads and tried to figure out the best routes and highways to get to the hospital. At this point, my mind was not able to figure out the map that was ahead of me or the road I was to take as a caregiver. Was I borrowing time or would it change for me?

Despite this long list of chores during the limited outdoor time we had, my mind was blowing things out of proportion. It refused to live in the moment no matter how hard I tried. Even though all I had was *now*, the moment was inevitable, I kept going back to the *past*. I was trying to stay in a time when all of this never happened. I often imagined a huge eraser in my hand to erase the present. I wanted to hold on to the moment of being in the outside world with her being free. The moment she was born and came into my arms, the moment she said mom for the first time, her first tooth, her first step, her first haircut. Then, suddenly out of nowhere, her first chemo entered our life. The time she entered my life until now was playing games just like the flickering lightbulb in a storm. This storm would make us stay indoors and build our immunity. All three of us to this new life.

Chapter 5 – The Warrior Who Painted Her Fight

We started our journey with the clinic visit where she would be treated. I had to be educated on how life would be for the coming months. While I was in the action zone, my husband had to concentrate on working. I often wondered how he managed to do that with so much going on in our lives. Her phase 2 of treatment started and lasted for one week. During this time, while still trying to settle into the new life, things started to feel heavy on my shoulders. The days were becoming more tiring emotionally. As she approached the end of her phase 2, she started to feel sad and tired as a lot was changing for her internally. But she never gave up on hope or her smile. Those two factors were enough for me to move forward to phase 3 of her treatment that would last for a minimum of 100 days. She showed me what a warrior she was. Her spirit to fight this and her internal strength to not give up is still magical for me.

The time in the hospital and at the apartment, as uncommon as it might sound, bonded us as a family. My husband's silence and our relationship became less of terms and more of feelings. Perhaps this happened as we understood the unspoken words and felt the pain we both were going through, but never talked about. We knew who needed a break and how each one of us had a very important role to play in this war.

In this journey, this was not the only bond I had formed. I had a connection with 16 other families who had a child admitted on the same floor. They had similar, if not more intense battles that they were fighting.

Chapter 5 – The Warrior Who Painted Her Fight

Every daybreak we would meet in the break-room to get our morning coffee and ask about the night before. Sometimes I would see a room empty, cleaned and disinfected, with a new name on the door. At that moment, I would be informed by the nurses that the warrior got wings and now was an angel. I witnessed four warriors taking the wings of an angel in my 100-day stay at the hospital. I had no courage at all to tell my little warrior what happened when she would ask for Ryan or Mathew. Nor could I contact the parents, as I was in a war (not sure, but hopeful) of my own destiny.

With several bumps along the road to the transplant, we finally reached the 100th day that every single family waits to celebrate. It is by far the first milestone that we look forward to. If she stayed infection free and her body had accepted the new treatment, it was time for us to head home; and yes we were ready. I was grateful and happy because it was like taking a newborn home once again. However, this time I had promised myself that I would take extra special care than I did the first time. The child life support and the nurses made this moment special for her.

As we packed her room where we stayed way over 100 days, it was time to get the instructions that seemed to never end. We had to learn the process of drawing blood and the do's and don'ts of our new life as she entered phase 4. At that point, her Oncologist came in and just said to us, "I would not worry about her transplant, but I would worry when she gets a driver's license!" These words comforted me for years to come. It took a big load off my shoulders and gave me wings to fly again.

Chapter 5 – The Warrior Who Painted Her Fight

As she stepped out of the room, she saw a huge surprise. Nurses, doctors and patients that were now family (perhaps more), all lined up on either side of the corridors to cheer for the warrior. As she passed by and said her goodbyes, she was showered with confetti, loud applause, horns and cheers that reminded us of what victory looks like. We had gratitude for everyone who played a role for this day to come.

As I stepped out of the final door, one of the nurses came to me and said, "Manu…just don't look back and tell the same to the warrior to never to look back either." With that said, I pressed the button that read *Push to Open* and took my princess home to enter the next phase of our lives.

Today, 12 years later, life still throws challenges at us now and then. We have side-effects of the war that we live with under a new normal. These challenges are not supposed to paralyze you; they're supposed to help you discover who you are. Often life gets me entangled in everyday actions, reactions and replay modes, but every day I start up again for it is a new day. I have to let go of the noise from the past to enjoy today's music. Janvi continues to paint for a cause, while we as her parents wish for her to go paint the world in color. Her first piece of art sold for $40 at a charity event benefiting Make-A-Wish Foundation. Last year she had a piece that went for $14000 making the total a little over $78,000 to date. The brush is still in her hand like the color of life.

And for me, when I sit down today with my morning tea, I revisit my strengths as a woman and a mother.

Chapter 5 – The Warrior Who Painted Her Fight

I know the only way to overcome fear is to be in the present and face it because fear is all about what that does not exist. Living with something that does not exist is insanity and it will drive anyone insane. My memory and the imagination of my mind caused fear in me that I learned to face as a mother. What I have today is her and my belief that we all have strength inside of us that time lets us unfold in different ways one day at a time.

- Manu Shahi

Chapter 5 – The Warrior Who Painted Her Fight

Chapter 5 – The Warrior Who Painted Her Fight

About the Author – Manu Shahi

Born and raised in North India, she moved to the United States in 1994. A successful businesswoman, educator, Ziglar Certified Speaker, and active community volunteer, Manu is living her dream of helping kids as a Certified Instructor.

She and her husband Sandeep are raising their daughter, Janvi in Flower Mound, Texas.

You can contact her at

shahimanu@verizon.net or 972.333.4663.

Chapter 5 – The Warrior Who Painted Her Fight

Chapter 6

What Are You Thinking
By John J. Caimano

"Everyone is in relationship building, everyone! That's because we all have family, friends and a work-life."

Life is all about relationships, business is all about relationships and if you're in the business world, (which everyone is in at some point in their life) then developing long deep relationships are as important as the nature of your business. Here's the truth about relationships: It is a conscious decision to build any relationship whether personal or business. You cannot fake a relationship. It has to be real.

Regarding business to business relationships, it's been said it's all about the list, the money is on the list. The truth is that the greatest asset of any business are the people. If you or your employees aren't building relationships among each other or with your clients, you will always be at the mercy of the next best opportunity.

So, what would I know about relationships…. I know a lot about relationships. I've been married 43 years, that's right 43 years! Of course, it was 43 different marriages of one year each.

Chapter 6 – What Are You Thinking?

Okay, the truth is that I have been married 43 years to the same great woman. There were some good times, some not so good times and there were many great times. Ups and downs are the nature of any relationship. One person says *don't sweat the small stuff because it's all small stuff* and the problem is that another person may say *I'm concerned about the small stuff because we all see issues at different levels.*

That reminds me of a joke. A man comes home from a hard day's work and asks his wife "What's for dinner?" She says "It's your choice. You can have beef Wellington, shrimp & lobster, crown roast of pork or I can cook."

Just about every relationship will have a difficult time and life is not about waiting for the difficulty to pass, it's about learning how to work through it. Relationship issues will come and go, the sky of life is full of turbulence as well; so we need to learn to fly through, being careful that our turbulent issues don't affect our relationships. Why? That's the nature of relationships. Just about all relationships will have turbulence. And again - All relationships take work!

There are Four Steps to Building Winning Relationships:

1. Develop integrity
2. Control your temper
3. Live the Golden Rule
4. Develop an encouraging environment

Chapter 6 – What Are You Thinking?

DEVELOP INTEGRITY

Integrity speaks to good character, fairness, sincerity, truthfulness and trustworthiness. There is strength and stability in integrity.

I was talking to a young man who just graduated from college. He recently got a sales position at a furniture store (a large regional chain). As they were training him, one of the points that the sales manager made to him was that **"Buyers are liars!"** I said what? I know that you are NOT kidding, but this is outrageous!! This is what they're teaching you?! Where is the Integrity? With integrity you have nothing to lose, you have nothing to fear since you have nothing to hide. Here's what Zig Ziglar said about integrity: "With integrity you will do the right thing, so you will have no guilt. With the fear and guilt removed you are free to BE and DO your BEST!"

How about creating some integrity by teaching the salesman an alternate close that would suggest an option for a better warranty in a higher line mattress? How about instead of questioning the integrity of the folks that you are trying to sell a mattress to (buyers are liars), build a relationship with them. Connect with them, find common ground. Build a relationship.
Relationships are built on:

KNOWING - LIKING - TRUSTING

How about instead of questioning the integrity of a potential client, you prove YOURS!
It didn't take my young friend but a few weeks for him to figure out that this was not a working environment that he wanted to be associated with.

Chapter 6 – What Are You Thinking?

I'm reminded of a time when I had the opportunity to deepen a relationship with one of my largest clients. I am a manufacturer's representative selling in a precast concrete niche market. My client called my cell phone late on a Saturday afternoon and told me that the factory had short-shipped his order and a crew was going to be on site first thing Monday morning and needed the missing items to get their day started. The good news was I had just enough products in my backyard to accommodate this situation. The bad news was that it was too late in the day to load the 1950 lbs. of product into my mid-size SUV. Compounding the situation, the next day, Sunday (the day I go to church), was also Father's Day. I explained to my wife what was going on. I told her that I had to make this delivery after church on Father's Day. She knew that if I was willing to give up family time on a day that celebrated family and fathers, that it was very important to me and our household that I load the SUV and make the one hour and forty-five-minute trip to make the delivery. I also had to explain that at 1950 lbs. the SUV was over loaded and couldn't have her ride shotgun, so I told her I'd be back in four and one-half to five hours.

Everything we do in life takes effort. You have to put something in, in order to get something out. I only kept product at my home for the occasion of a small incident, maybe 600 lbs. of product wrapped in moving blankets to keep from ruining the interior of the SUV. I was very much stressed about making this trip with 1950 lbs. loaded.

The fact that a bear jumped out in front of me and the load shifted to squeeze me in the driver's seat didn't help. I did finally arrive home safely five hours later.

Chapter 6 – What Are You Thinking?

Ultimately, it all paid off. Some months later I signed a contract with the client for $1,113,000.00 which earned me in excess of ninety thousand dollars that year; I knew why I invested in the relationship so heavily.

CONTROL YOUR TEMPER

Just about everyone knows that emotional discussions are just that, EMOTIONAL. In order to develop deep relationships, good working relationships, we need to have thoughtful responses and not react in an EMOTIONAL or IMPULSIVE way. John Maxwell (The nation's premier authority on leadership) says, "If a person doesn't govern his temper, his temper will govern him."

You can imagine that after being married 43 years, my wife and I have had a few discussions. My heritage would suggest that all discussions would be and/or should be LOUD. I am ashamed to say that there have been a few loud discussions. Sometimes things go wrong, and when they do, some people think that they can get their best result by shouting at the other person. Should an incident arise in a relationship, it is best to approach the situation at its earliest opportunity. The sooner a situation is addressed the easier it is to patch. In a similar light, if you are in a heated discussion on the phone and the other person is using profanity, hang up. Anytime I had employees, they were instructed to do just that! Hang up! Additionally, if I'm on the phone and the client is venting his frustration and they come to a pause, I ask, "Are you finished?" It's like the Dog Whisperer giving a little snap correction. Now we can get on with solving the issue.

Chapter 6 – What Are You Thinking?

Loud conversations are mostly non-productive. However, I will say that I have had to say a few times in some important conversations "Do not mistake my calm demeanor for weakness!"

LIVE THE GOLDEN RULE

Do unto others as you would have them do unto you. Treat others as you would like to be treated. I grew up on the streets of NYC, the Borough of Brooklyn to be exact. At that time, the Borough of Brooklyn was the 5th largest city in the United States. I was a street smart kid. The Golden Rule on the streets was "Do unto others as you would have them do, only do it FIRST!" I'm proud to say that my parents worked hard at instilling core values in me that reflected the proper application. The Golden Rule says: How can I help you? Do I treat you with respect? Do I properly communicate with you? Am I conscious enough to make advance warnings or changes? Have I expressed my appreciation for your efforts today? Do I demonstrate my appreciation for your friendship? Applying the Golden Rule says sometimes we have to do the right thing instead of doing things right.

A friend of mine was building a new house. When the excavator was digging the hole for the basement foundation they noticed some water in one corner of the hole. An engineer was called in to make an evaluation of the soil to make sure the soils were appropriate to hold the house without sinking. The engineer gave the "all is okay" and the work proceeded. About a week or two later the wet spot in the corner became eight inches of water in the foundation. They had hit a spring. Here's the problem. The house will be thirty-two feet tall when finished.

Chapter 6 – What Are You Thinking?

The town ordinance required that the house be no more than thirty-two feet high, but my friend needed to raise the basement floor; therefore raising the first floor and ultimately changing the height of the house to thirty-four feet tall. Okay so here's where doing the right thing vs. doing things right comes in. The town official realized that if he held my friend to the letter of the law that it would result in pumping the water to the side yard and would eventually find its way onto the street. Taking into consideration at the very least, freezing conditions in the winter and the mess that would be, a variance was granted to alleviate the situation. "Doing the right thing vs. doing things right."

DEVELOP AN ENCOURAGING ENVIRONMENT

Andrew Carnegie once said, "It's amazing what you can accomplish if you don't care who gets the credit." It's important to maintain a positive frame of mind. It's important to develop your positive self. It's important to be a chronic encourager. People should always be able to say, "She's always so nice to me" or "He is such a great guy."

My wife says that my mom would even have something nice to say about Charlie Manson! Certainly she exaggerates when she says that. My mom would say, "Look how nice he ties his shoes…" My mom always had a positive frame of mind hardly a negative comment ever came out of her mouth. I grew up in a low-income household. It was Mom, Dad, my older brother (we're only 21 months apart) and me in a one-bedroom apartment. Then my kid sister came along when I was seven. We lived in that apartment until I was eleven and the house was really crowded.

Chapter 6 – What Are You Thinking?

Somehow, my mom found a way to have a party as often as we could on a Sunday afternoon. "She would say, "Let's have a party!"

She would scrape the pennies out of the bottom of her pocketbook. It was just enough to buy a family size bottle of soda (Coca Cola please) and pint of ice cream. This was another example to me of not only developing an encouraging attitude, but how to build an encouraging family atmosphere.

I am sure that it takes the same amount of effort to develop positive comments about someone than negative ones. Think positive thoughts about yourself and others.

Tom Ziglar, proud son of Zig Ziglar, said "The fastest way to success is to replace bad habits with good habits." This particular comment was made when Tom was answering questions at the end of a speech. I am mostly sure that the person who asked the question, asked with financial success as the motive. However, the statement can be made about relationships as well. "Replace bad habits with good ones." Replace bad comments with positive ones. Regardless of your goals, regardless of your current depth of relationships, being a chronic learner, a lifelong learner helps to re-set your attitude about relationships and your attitude is your STRENGTH in all relationships!

Make the changes you need to make to be the best possible person you can be. You will see how the world of relationships changes around you.

Chapter 6 – What Are You Thinking?

Customer Service is a Lost Art

I was on the phone not too long ago with Roy. I have great respect for Roy. Roy has more than 25 years of service in the same niche industry that I am associated with. We quite often have had heavy discussions as to who is the best salesman in the business (it is a long running joke). He is a wealth of technical information and sells from that standpoint, as well as building great relationships. When I first came on the scene, Roy was the national sales leader. Two years in, I was recognized as the national sales leader (with less than three years of experience), that's when the questions started and the banter began! I moved on to be the national sales leader for six years in a row and in the top three for ten years. I always told him that he was the best and he always told me that I was the best. I made several multi-million dollar sales over those years and earned a deep six figure income for my efforts. When other sales people would ask me how I did it, I would say, "I don't sell anything, I build relationships."

That in fact, was the very point of our conversation. He was in a sales meeting a few days prior and told the group that there wasn't anyone in our niche industry who gave better customer service than John Caimano. I was surprised that I would still be a household name since I had long moved on from the manufacturer he was selling for. Then Roy says to me "Customer service is a lost Art." Yes, I agreed, customer service is a lost art.

Recently my wife and I walked into our local club store where the greeter was sitting on an old office chair and could

Chapter 6 – What Are You Thinking?

hardly say hello with a frown. I think to myself this is customer service at its simplest level and it is being as poorly done as possible. This is where my relationship is supposed to begin! Posting a greeter at the front door is in its nature an extended hand and the very, very beginning of your store relationship. Your experience at the store should start with a smile and snap. When we were leaving the store, I handed the young lady my receipt so she could count the items in our cart. She never left her seat! There was no way she could count all the items in the cart (good thing I have been accused of being too honest), because she couldn't see them all from her line of sight. As we walked away I commented to my wife what a great experience that was and that she was the face of the store.

Now I don't know if the woman at the front door had a medical issue that prevented her from standing to look at all the items in the cart, but I know from experience that even when I'm not in the correct state of mind I can pretend all is well and smile. If it was my job to stand, to see and count all the items in the cart, then that's what I would do. This was not the first time that I had encountered this young lady at the front door. I continued to tell my wife, as we loaded the car, that she was in the wrong line of work. That whoever placed her at the door was equally mistaken. I thought, *can you please, please put an extrovert at the front door? Someone with a genuine smile who loves to interact with the people he or she greets. Someone that might just might remember a regular customer's name, and even if he or she has life issues, they leave them at the threshold of their home.*

Chapter 6 – What Are You Thinking?

What is more curious is that the practice of having a dull and unengaged greeter is epidemic at many retailers. How about "Welcome, we're glad you stopped in today. Can I direct you to a particular item? Don't forget if you need additional direction I'll be here." The introverts visiting may not necessarily appreciate the greeting, but they would know that someone is there if they need help finding an item. The extroverts will quickly glance at the name tag and engage in a short conversation. The side note here, is that if you are engaging with someone and they are wearing a name tag, then call them by their name. You will be surprised at how well the encounter goes when you use their name.

Now I'm all worked up. My wife knows to just let me go when I say, "Don't even get me started on telephone systems." What in the world are companies thinking I say to her? I don't want to talk to a computer, press one, press five and press seven, so I can press zero. I want to speak to the person who can get me to the person that I want to speak to. What are the leaders thinking? We don't need to build or maintain a relationship with the person on the phone. How can I frustrate the caller? Let me see if I can frustrate our client or potential client enough so they will hang up and take their business elsewhere? How many times do I hear someone say, that they wasted forty-five minutes on hold? Additionally, don't have your phones answered on another continent by someone who speaks terrible English and says his name is Jim (wink). The expense of customer service, guest relations and customer relations is a cost of doing business. It needs to be taken in the most serious way.

Chapter 6 – What Are You Thinking?

Recently, I have noticed some insurance companies who are chasing market share, have started to figure this out. People want to engage with people, and in particular, when there is an issue, they want to develop an intimate relationship without any hassle. In the same light there are some company leaders who are mistaken about how important the relationship is between their sales staff and their customers. I think back many years ago to one of my first jobs. The company's switch board was shared by a wonderful mother and daughter team. They operated as the receptionists as well. When clients came to visit, they already knew them from speaking with them when they dialed in. The clients were always pleased to meet either of the voices that pleasantly greeted them on the phone. It was an experience to remember. A bright spot in everyone's day they were. Please put a bright extroverted smiling face at the front door, a bright live and cheery voice at the forefront of your telephone system. It will pay huge dividends.

Last year for Christmas, when searching for a gift for my wife, I decided that I would like to get her a new set of pots and pans. I was solicited by a major retailer and I saw the perfect set. I consulted with her and she agreed that after 43 years with the same pots that it would be nice to have new ones. Whenever I purchase anything I research the quality and buy the best product I can afford. If you want to purchase a good set of pots and pans they are expensive. This particular set was made in America and I liked the idea of supporting an American manufacturer. We made the decision to purchase a 16-piece set.

Chapter 6 – What Are You Thinking?

The story really begins about nine months later, my wife asked me to cook some onions on the grill to keep the smell out of the house. No Problem.

Twenty minutes later, when carrying the large sauté pan back into the house, I discovered that the pan is defective. My wife agrees that one of the pans she may have used two or three times is defective. We take a trip down to the mall with the pan in tote and bring it back to the store. We are greeted by a clerk as we enter the store who said, "We don't accept returns on defective pots. You have to send it back to the manufacturer. I have their phone number right here." The first thing I think is: I'm standing in your store with a defective pot that was sold through your corporation. How about "Oh, I'm sorry folks for the inconvenience this has caused you. Please give me your contact information and we will have the manufacturer replace it."

Do you understand that this statement in itself will drop my stress level and when you call me to tell me the replacement has arrived; I will be in your store again? (Have you seen our new line of spatulas?) It is much easier to sell to an existing customer than develop a new one.

We then called the manufacturer's customer service and sent the pot to the requested location. On the phone, my wife was told by the customer care representative that it would take seven to ten days to process the repair/replacement request. Five weeks later, a package arrived at our home. I called my wife to ask her if she was expecting a package.

Chapter 6 – What Are You Thinking?

She says "It's my sauté pan." Wow, I had forgotten all about it needing to be repaired. She said "Yep, I had to call them several times to get them to ship it out." I told her, "Okay I'll check it out." Three minutes later I'm on the phone with her again. "They sent the wrong pan… They sent a frying pan…" Three minutes later she calls me and says "Pack it up. I have a return authorization number and bring it to UPS to have it shipped again." We are now six weeks into the process and still don't have a replacement.

The customer care representative supervisor is unavailable and has not called back. The situation is still not resolved as I write this paragraph. Sadly, we now have mixed emotions, not only about the quality of the manufacturers' products, but also about the care for resolving issues. We probably would recommend the product, but with caution.

What a difference a day makes. As it turns out, the customer service manager called my wife a day later, and as I would expect, my wife spoke to him in a clear, calm way. The good news is that he was very apologetic for the weeks that passed for the mix up and he sent her a new-in-box sauté pan, next day delivery. It restored our faith in the American way of life and now she is a very happy cook. This leads me to my final note:

One of my clients recently went on vacation in North Carolina; he told me it was a bit of a surprise. The surprise was that his wife had picked a shore destination in a warmer climate and it wasn't Miami Beach.

Chapter 6 – What Are You Thinking?

Upon his return, he was overflowing with Southern Hospitality. He just couldn't believe how friendly, nice and genuine the people were. As he was speaking about his experience, I couldn't help but think that Southern Hospitality was actually alive and well right in our backyards. I was thinking "Have you ever gone to eat at a Chick-fil-A restaurant?" They greet you like long lost family who they missed and loved and when you say, "Thank you," they say "My pleasure."

Chick-fil-A got its humble beginnings in Atlanta, Georgia and the founders not only want to continue the tradition of Southern Hospitality as they grow their franchise system nationally, but also close on Sundays so the employees can have family time.

So as it is Roy, Customer Service is an art to be practiced, but is not yet lost.
- John J. Caimano

Chapter 6 – What Are You Thinking?

Chapter 6 – What Are You Thinking?

Meet The Author – John Caimano

John J Caimano is a successful awarding winning manufacturer's representative to the construction industry. Over the past 18 years, John has taken a virtually unknown product and successfully increased product awareness in the state of New Jersey, developing it into a multi-million dollar business. As a national award winner John has been one of the top three, sales incentive winners seven consecutive years ahead of over 165 other representatives. After leaving corporate America and then becoming an entrepreneur, John has gained his sales and marketing experience over the last thirty years which has given him a keen sense, he says; "I think differently, I don't sell anything, I build relationships."

As a firm believer in continuing education, and following Zig Ziglar for forty years, John has become a Ziglar Certified Legacy Trainer. John is Certified to Train: Leadership; Goal Setting; Relationship Building; Building the Best You and Curriculum based Coaching. John thrives on new business challenges and not just to succeed; but to develop as many relationships as possible. John develops and encourages people so they can be the best that they can be no matter what their lot in life. John lives in the beautiful hills of Hunterdon County, New Jersey with his wife of 43 years and their faithful companion Jack, their standard poodle.

John J. Caimano
Intended Impact LLC
Ziglar Legacy Certified Speaker, Trainer, Coach & Author
john@intendedimpact.com

Chapter 6 – What Are You Thinking?

Chapter 7

Start by Changing Yourself
By Todd Pagel

It was the first Sunday of 2016 when I came across a social media post from someone who appeared to be extremely troubled. The details they described disturbed me, but it was the comment at the end that stood out the most. After reading it, the words stuck with me heavily. She was suggesting that she should end her life. I'm not a huge fan of Facebook, Twitter, or any of the other social media sites for my own reasons. But, I do understand the power social media has when it comes to many things like promoting business, reconnecting with old friends and the like, but in this case, it just might have saved a life.

Needless to say after reading the post, I immediately took action so that the appropriate people could take action to help this person.

That same Monday, I boarded a plane back to Dallas. After spending some time with my family over the holidays back in Wisconsin, it was time to get back to the office. As usual, my parents were overly generous to all of us, especially to the grandkids.

Chapter 7 – Start by Changing Yourself

My parents are incredible people and over the years, we have had many good conversations about society's declining values, most notably those of their grandchildren, my nephews. The discussions are always the same and the conclusions always consistent. We all agree, the world is increasingly becoming a messed up place. That is always followed by the statement, "It is what it is, but is there really anything we can do about it?" **The answer, of course, is no... or is it?"**

Because I travel regularly for my job, I have the fortune, or what has recently become the misfortune of being allowed to board the plane when the first group of passengers is called. I call that privilege the red badge of courage because I have had to regularly put up with the "Self-Centered" & "Entitled" society. For those of you that travel frequently, know what I'm talking about.

The return trip to Dallas wasn't anything out of the ordinary. Upon hearing the call for my group to board, I took my place in line and proceeded to the plane. Unfortunately, the plane was full and my spoiled backside wasn't granted the upgrade. After relishing in self-pity for a minute (shame on me), I took my seat which was located at seat 8A. Supposedly by Delta airlines standards, this seat has been seriously misnamed as "Economy Comfort." Maybe the economy part was right, but there was nothing comfortable about it.

Given that it was Monday; old Murphy's Law was fully operational.

Chapter 7 – Start by Changing Yourself

I looked up from my book, to see a rather large gentleman, to be kind, coming toward me carrying two items anyone could easily assess were not going to take their place in the overhead compartment without a major battle.

I'm sure you are reading this faster than I am typing it, so you know exactly what happened next. Yep, after holding up the line for the other boarding passengers for at least a couple minutes, while he made sure he took care of himself, he sits in seat 7A, right in front of me. What do you think happened next? Yep, as soon as the wheels left the runway, seat 7A fully reclines. For the next three hours, I proceeded to get an unappealing close-up of the back of this man's head, unable to even deploy the tray table to work on my tablet. Another three hours of bliss.

Having been a victim of this kind of experience too many times, I quickly engaged my back-up plan and listened to three hours of motivation and goal setting by one of my mentors and quickly was reminded of why I am here on this earth. For any doubters that may no longer be listening to my airplane example, chances are you have never had to catch a connecting flight. The flight attendant asks for people that do not have a connecting flight, to graciously let those with a close connecting flight deplane first. I have traveled over a million miles, and I sadly report, I have never had anyone who was sitting in front of me let me deplane before them, and as a direct result, I have missed a lot of connecting flights. "Self-Centered" & "Entitled?" Yes, I think so.

Chapter 7 – Start by Changing Yourself

Despite what the constitution says, all men, and for the politically correct, all people are not created equal (in my opinion). Of course, we are all given the same unalienable rights, but we are far from being created equal. We are all given the same opportunities, but we are not created equal. I cannot pass a football like Tom Brady. As much as I try, I cannot create the next operating system like Bill Gates did. No, we are not all created equal, but we all are given the same opportunities by our creator to accomplish everything in life we want if we are willing to apply ourselves and work towards it.

Considering that I believe that all people are not created equal, the next time you have an opportunity to board a plane, take that opportunity and become a people watcher. You will witness classic examples of how self-centered and entitled our society has become by observing the people boarding and deplaning a plane. As Mom and Dad asked, "It is what it is, but is there really anything we can do about it?" **Of course the answer is no… or is it**?

On a side note, the next time you have the opportunity to fly, carry a couple Hersey's Kisses with you and give them to the crew as you board the plane. You will be amazed at what happens. Who do you think will get the most attention on that flight? Nope, it's not the jerk in first class, it will be the person sitting where I am. Always remember, treat people as if they have a sign on their back that says, "MAKE ME FEEL IMPORTANT," and they will make you feel incredible.

Chapter 7 – Start by Changing Yourself

About five years ago I was in need of a smaller vehicle for running back and forth to work. The commute was 35 miles one way, and an F-150 pick-up truck that gets 13-14 mpg, well you can do the math. It so happened that my financial planner was selling a car called a Pontiac Vibe. I had never even heard of a Pontiac Vibe, but after doing my research and given the price, it fit perfectly into the equation I was looking for. Incidentally, I would advise against becoming too good of friends with your financial advisors, especially one that wants to sell you something, but that's another story.

After doing my research and given the negotiated price, I purchased the car, and it has since served me and now my brother well. Once I started using the car, a strange thing happened. Everyone began driving Pontiac Vibes. It seemed like everywhere I turned, people were driving Pontiac Vibes. For a brief selfish minute, my ego tried to convince me that I had a serious influence in the community to convince all these people to drive Pontiac Vibes. Of course that was ridiculous, but there was a strong lesson to be learned from that experience. They tell me this is known as reticular activation. I'm not really sure who "they" are, but "they" always appear to have all the answers to everything.

No matter who you are, or what experiences you have had in life, there are certain things ingrained into your subconscious mind. Whether it was a smell (Olfactory Activation), a song (Audible Activation) or any of the other senses that activate a memory, it is so important to

Chapter 7 – Start by Changing Yourself

understand the power this has on changing behavior. This is extremely important for answering Mom and Dad's question. "It is what it is, but is there really anything we can do about it?" **The answer, of course, is no… or is it?**

About 25 years ago, someone who cared deeply about me and where I was headed dragged me kicking and screaming to a success seminar. With everything in my being, I tried to get out of going, but thank God I was unsuccessful in doing so. The featured speaker was this guy named Zig Ziglar. My career had already taken off, and I was quickly climbing the corporate ladder. Out of respect for my friend, I reluctantly went to the seminar.

To say my life has never been the same would be one of the greatest understatements ever made. It only took about five minutes and for the next two hours (which felt like only 15 minutes) I listened and learned a philosophy that I bought into hook line and sinker, as they say in Wisconsin. Going into that seminar, I thought I was "ALL THAT" and no one named Zig Ziglar was going to teach me anything. However, Mr. Ziglar said something that I will never forget. He said, "If your goal is to have a great quality of life and all you get out of it is a higher standard of living, you are a failure." It was at that point that I realized I wasn't smarter than my Mom and Dad, like most kids feel about their parents in this day and age, "Self-Centered" & "Entitled." This philosophy is simple and timeless. Whatever you put into your mind, it will be returned to you exponentially, good or bad.

Chapter 7 – Start by Changing Yourself

For the last 25 years, a day has not gone by in my life that I do not put at least one hour of the good, the clean, the pure, the powerful, and the positive messages into my mind. What happens is you start to clearly see those Pontiac Vibes everywhere, but this time it's not a car, it's:

Integrity	Team Player
Honesty	Optimistic
Discipline	Focused
Enthusiastic	Decisive
Motivated	Positive Mental Attitude
Persistent	Respectful
Energetic	Sincere
Gratitude	Affectionate
Dependable	Loyal
Honor	Service
Commitment	Rectitude

So what is the answer to Mom and Dad's question? "It is what it is, but is there really anything we can do?" Of course there is. The first step is to start putting the good stuff in, and then and only then can you expect to get the good stuff out. Yes, the answer is really that easy, but by no means close to simple. Wait, it is simple, it simply needs to be implemented. Whether you are running a multi-national corporation, a small business, a family household, or your own personal life, EXECUTION is the key. If you aren't willing to take the first step, you will never take the second or the third. Commit to at least begin putting good things into your mind.

Chapter 7 – Start by Changing Yourself

More importantly, start putting it into the next generation. The last thing we need is more gamers, who know how to rob, steal, and shoot on a video game. What message does that send? Instead, fill their heads with the good, the clean, and powerful, and the positive, and they will indeed accomplish everything else they want, and help us become the United States we once were.

A "Self-Centered" & "Entitled" society is really ugly, just like those people on the plane.

When I look back at that initial post I read at the beginning of this story, I realize that self-destructive behavior is all too common in our country today. I have known kids who were excellent students until addiction took control of their life. I have seen people who are stunningly beautiful lose it all to the desires of their addiction. After years of abuse, they look terrible. From stained rotting teeth to a body that looks similar to my grandfather's declining body as he died of lung cancer. The physical evidence is clear.

Although the sadness of the physical tolls the addiction has taken is apparent, it is the mental aspect of the addiction that is so hard to tolerate and swallow.

I thought about this person not being a failure, but maybe they were failed. I wanted to learn a lesson from this and therefore, I am committed to making it my biggest lesson learned. I will commit to getting through to people I know who are destroying their lives.

Chapter 7 – Start by Changing Yourself

I pray every day it's not too late to have a positive influence on someone's life. Imagine if they were given the same gift I was all those years ago. Faith in God, a set of parents that instilled in me the true lessons of life, and finally, good friends that took you to meet that mentor that taught you a philosophy that can indeed, change the world, but only if you start by changing yourself.

So Mom and Dad, yes, there is something we can do for a society that is "Self-Centered" & "Entitled." We can do the exact thing you did with me. Thank you for everything you have done for me, you will always be my parents, my best friends, and the reason I am who I am.

To every parent, every boss, every teacher, every government official, everyone in any walk of life, who comes into contact with people, remember the first step is simple and yes very easy. Read, listen, and surround yourself with sound, strong and positive people. The changes you see and experience will be exponential. A good place to start would be "See You At The Top" by Zig Ziglar, at least until my book is finished.

God Bless You and God Bless the United States of America.

- Todd Pagel

Chapter 7 – Start by Changing Yourself

Chapter 7 – Start by Changing Yourself

Meet The Author – Todd Pagel

Todd Pagel was born in Central Wisconsin. Early on, Todd's parents instilled in him the values, character and discipline he talks about in this book. Whether it was a strong faith-based education or the value of "never giving up" when attempting to accomplish anything. Whether it was participating in sports (back then, they didn't give you a participant award), or applying for a job, Todd's Mom and Dad implanted in his head that you never give up.

Throughout his career, Todd applied the principles his parents and grandparents instilled and practiced. That produced success in every aspect of his career, which has provided him with the avenues to give back significantly. Todd continues to utilize the tools he was given by his parents.

About 25 years ago he met the man that helped him put all the pieces together, Zig Ziglar. With a strong foundation, now combined with a strong philosophy, Todd has begun the next chapter of his life. Every day Todd confirms Zig's biggest promise. "You can have everything in life you want, if you will just help enough other people get what they want." Todd has a distinct way of helping others to put the good stuff in. Join Todd and the other authors in this book, and together we will all see you at the top.

2401 Franklin Street, Wausau, WI 54403 ♦ 715.574.5776 ♦ LinkedIn.com/pub/todd-pagel/15/97a/a98

toddpagel@msn.com

Chapter 7 – Start by Changing Yourself

Chapter 8

Overcoming Adversity
Get Back Up Even Stronger
By Jahbari McLennan

My name is Jahbari McLennan. I have lived the first part of my life chasing after football and trying to make it into the NFL. You could not tell me for one second that I was not going into the NFL because I worked hard and I was proud of my results. I am going to give you a quick snapshot of one of my highlights when I was playing football in college, then as I made a transition to life after I graduated from school.

When I graduated, I had shoe boxes full of football letters from big schools. The only thing I wanted to do was get a scholarship from one of them, so my parents did not have to pay for me to go to school. When signing day came for me at John H. Reagan High School in Austin, Texas, the only offer I had was to a community college called Trinity Valley in Athens, Texas. Just in case you were wondering about the population difference, you could take 50 times the population of Athens and it would still fall short of the total population of Austin in 2006.

I built some great relationship with players and coaches, and one of those relationships was with Terrence Murphy. He was more than just a coach to me. He became my mentor. He did not only teach me a lot about football (drafted 2nd round to the Green Bay Packers in 2005), he was an example

Chapter 8 – Overcoming Adversity

of how to live out your faith on and off the field. That was very profound for me as a teenager becoming a man in today's world.

Picture yourself waking up for 5 am workouts with two practices in one day. Having a heat index in the high 80s and seeing your teammates with full body cramps, not being able to move. Teammates would carry each other to an ice bath in order to help each other gain control of their own bodies again. That was a highlight of my daily reality when I reached my first goal of getting a scholarship to a Division 1 college football team. The first game I played was not only one of my biggest games in my college career, but also that in the University's books. We beat Texas A&M and the 12th man. The entire student body at A&M is referred to as the 12th man, due to their boisterous cheering. It was almost as if they were on the field with you playing. Man, that was an unforgettable win and so was the day of September 13, 2008. This was a day I will never forget.

September 13, 2008, was the day we played Southern Mississippi Golden Eagles. The day started off with the team's normal day rituals: breakfast, meetings, warming up and pep talks leading up to the game. Evening hit and it was game time. I was on the kickoff return team and my main assignment was to pick up the first block that came down field if I did not catch the football. I was supposed to block the first person speeding down field that was going to attempt to tackle the person who had the ball. The guy on the opposing team firing down the field had not been touched by any of my teammates. He seemed as if he was moving a hundred miles per hour.

Chapter 8 – Overcoming Adversity

He was going towards the person with the ball and I just happened to be in his way, or should I say in the correct position to block. So, as I set up to block, I planted myself and put my head down while he was coming full speed. He leaned his shoulder down and went straight into the side of my helmet and knocked me out! Instantly, I fell and was put to sleep in the middle of Red Wolf Stadium (now known as Centennial Bank Stadium). If you were to ask me what I was thinking, close your eyes right now and what you see is what I remember seeing that night, absolute darkness!

When I finally started to regain consciousness, I realized I was on a stretcher being carried into an ambulance. In my head, I knew something bad had happened and I needed to go to the hospital, but I wasn't in a state of mind to vividly remember all that happened. As the paramedics were trying to help me regain consciousness, one gentleman asked me a question I will never forget: "What is the name of the team you are playing?" he asked. Now, I knew the Southern Mississippi mascot was a golden eagle, as I had seen a picture of their mascot. However, I couldn't recall the words "golden eagle" in my head. I also knew the longer I took to respond to his question, he would assume that my condition was serious. So, the first thing that finally came out of my mouth after ten seconds of thinking was "yellow bird." My response resulted in a rapid rush of getting me to the hospital to ensure I was not in any danger health-wise.

We all have been knocked down to the point where we haven't grasped or fully understood our purpose in life, what we are doing with our lives and why we are where we are in life.

Chapter 8 – Overcoming Adversity

So let's start with simply defining the word *"Purpose."* According to Webster, a purpose is the aim or intention of something. It is also the feeling of being determined to do or achieve something and lastly the reason WHY.

You can't discover something from nothing; you have to be informed first. Simon Sinek said it best when he talked about how people don't care *what* you do until they care about *why* you do it. I was listening to one of Zig Ziglar's audio discs and he was asking the audience questions. One of the questions he asked was, "How many of you are currently in a field other than the one you earned a degree in?" I can tell that a lot of people raised their hands because he then said, "People, we've got to have goals in life." He makes a great point and in this book, I am going to walk through what it means to have goals. We get fooled into the "what" instead of the "why." We always want to have the money, cars, clothes, jewelry, title, position and the list goes on. If someone asked you "What is your purpose in life?" and you responded with, "To purchase a brand new Range Rover, hit the lottery, or buy a house in a particular neighborhood," what happens after you achieve getting those material things? Even though those are nice things to have, we cannot take them with us once we face death.

I have the honor of being a Sales Manager at a car dealership here in Jonesboro, Arkansas. One of my responsibilities is to hire salespeople and train them to be selling machines. One particular interview that has stayed memorable in my mind was an interview I had with a truck driver who had come in to apply for one of the sales positions here at the dealership. As I was doing the interview, I asked him why he would be a great fit for the job.

Chapter 8 – Overcoming Adversity

He responded by saying he was a truck driver for years and wanted to try sales because he'd never done it before. I continued to ask several questions and noticed that he wasn't talking very much. As you well know, salespeople have to be able to hold a decent conversation. I pressed on, conversing with him to allow him the chance to prove himself. It wasn't until I got to a specific question that I lost it in my head and his chances were now slim to none. I asked him what his purpose was in life and he replied with four words, "To get this job." Now, let me remind you he was applying for a sales job. He said very little and expected to get this job. Needless to say, I'm sure you figured out that the gentleman didn't get the job, as he wasn't a good fit for our company. I also saw a sad reality; people hop around from job to job looking, with no purpose or understanding, why they want the job. It was clear the guy just wanted to be in sales to try it out. If you know that you're applying for a job only to try it, how are you convincing anyone or yourself that it is the job for you?

Anyone in an executive position can tell you that the interview example mentioned above doesn't provoke one to hire a person that gives such answers. Reason being, it doesn't show the executive (who in this case, was me) that you will be committed to doing the job with purpose and do it well. *"Giving it a try"* gives the idea of the option to give up. That wasn't what I was looking for.

Punit Renjen, the Chairman of one of the top global auditing and consulting firms, emphasizes my point beautifully when he stated in an interview with Bruce Rogers (Forbes Staff) that...

Chapter 8 – Overcoming Adversity

Rogers: "Building a purpose focused culture is also not just about supporting social responsibility activities."
Renjen: "It first comes from treating customers well. It's not about transactions, but about building a relationship that exceeds expectation. My goal is to change the conversation about what makes companies succeed."

What he's saying is true. When we don't understand our purpose, then we live an aimless life that will not only mess up the business side of life, but your personal life as well. If your purpose does not reflect who you are, then you will produce bad or no fruit at all. Jesus explains it this way in Luke 6:43-44 (*NKJV*), "For a good tree does not bear bad fruit, nor does a bad tree bear good fruit. For every tree is known by its own fruit." Have you ever looked at an orange tree and wondered why it would not grow an apple? If you have, I will start praying for you because it does not matter how hard you wonder, that orange tree will always be an orange tree.

What would you do for free? When we look at just the financial award of something, it can be hard to determine whether you will do that same work for free. Everyone cannot do all their work for free and I understand that in today's world. I just want you to imagine with me; If we lived in a world where there was no such thing as money, but a world simply of service, what would you do? Would you offer your service in something you would or wouldn't enjoy doing? Would you be a garbage man if you enjoyed teaching a little league football team more? (No offense to the hard-working garbage men and women that take care of me every Friday - keep up the good work).

Chapter 8 – Overcoming Adversity

Which line of work would you give your 100% effort to that would make you reflect and be proud of? These questions allow you to be honest with yourself because you would have to live with that job. And don't forget, whatever job you pick, if you didn't make the necessary changes to do better, you would be stuck with for the rest of your life. Thus, I am sure you would put more effort into the choice that you would be more passionate about.

Being honest with yourself is one of, if not the hardest things any human being can do. It starts at a young age. I am currently taking care of my two nieces: Kyndle, who just turned three and McKenley, who is one. They were playing in their room and I was in the kitchen cleaning up. All of a sudden, Kyndle came up to my left side with her hands behind her back, looking at the paper towels. She spoke very softly and asked me, "Uncle Jahbari, can I have a napkin please?" Now at this moment, I was wondering why she needed a napkin if she was playing in her room. I noticed her hands behind her back. They were wet with a little foam around them. Her birthday had just passed and I recalled her receiving a bubble blower as one of her presents. I did not want her to open it without me or my wife assisting her because she would make a mess. I realized what she had done and I went to investigate.

I asked her, "Why are your hands wet?" She tilted her head down a little, but did not say anything. So, I asked her again, "Why are your hands wet?" As she started to say I don't know, I stopped her in her sentence and told her she would not get in trouble if she told the truth. I also told her that she would get in trouble if she lied. I squatted down and told her to look at me and tell me the truth.

Chapter 8 – Overcoming Adversity

You could tell it was hard for her to say, but she came out and said it, "I was playing with the bubbles and they spilled." As a proud Uncle, I got her a napkin and praised her for telling the truth. I gave her a hug and said thank you for telling the truth. She now had a smile on her face. I then kindly told her to go clean up her mess. We took some napkins in the bathroom. There was a small trail from the carpet to the bathroom floor and from the bathroom floor to the bathroom sink. There were also little pieces of paper on the floor from the package she opened. I was not as mad at her because she had been honest with me, but I did make her clean up her mess. Being honest with ourselves doesn't necessarily make the consequences of our actions disappear. We still have to take responsibility and deal with the consequences of the choices we make. No one is to be blamed but you and me. My little niece may not have known that telling the truth would pay off in the future, but I know it will. She was happy she didn't get into trouble for telling the truth and she was also happy to clean up her mess. Now, I will say that her little sister would not have been as willing to clean up her own mess, but she would have no choice in that matter because she made the mess.

A few points I want to make from these stories: We learn at a young age to tell the truth or not to tell the truth. Also, regardless if we tell the truth or not, we still have to take responsibility for the consequences of our choices. My niece told the truth, but she still had to clean up her mess. It is hard to find a purpose in life when you are not being true to yourself.

As I have learned from football, you have to work hard at anything worth having.

Chapter 8 – Overcoming Adversity

You must carry integrity with you because the more your word can be trusted, the less you have to worry about people doubting you. This will always lead you to your *why* in life: *Why* are you working hard? *Why* should you not try something, but aim to make something happen? *Why* do you need to have a purpose in life? Are you ready to get knocked down a little to get back up even stronger? If so, you will enjoy every day of your life knowing your direction and purpose!

- Jahbari McLennan

Chapter 8 – Overcoming Adversity

Chapter 8 – Overcoming Adversity

Meet The Author – Jahbari McLennan

My name is Jahbari McLennan. I was born in Houston, Texas, Dec. 8, 1987. I spent part of my life in Houston and the other part in Austin, Texas. I have one sibling and she is older than me, so I was the baby.

Sports was a huge part of my life and took up most of my time. In addition, it allowed me to stay focused instead of being distracted by other activities going on around me. Football became my favorite sport and I realized I wanted to go all the way to college and play. I had a chance to meet my pretty lady in college as she was a college athlete as well. We both still live in the city where we graduated, Jonesboro, Arkansas.

Chapter 8 – Overcoming Adversity

Chapter 9

Manifest Magnificence
with The Power of You
By Melody Tune

Do you believe you've accomplished everything you ever wanted in this life? In the past, were you able to see yourself in the future and now realize you are exactly where you envisioned you'd be?

A few short years ago I reflected on what my own life meant to me. It seemed quite ordinary, I thought, but now I see myself as being ... extraordinary.
Why?
Some of us have been conditioned to believe we are ordinary, as I did, not so long ago, or believe you're not good enough. Yet our creator has engineered us to be great. If your parents didn't tell you how great you are, I will! I know it to be the truth - my truth - and it can be your truth too.
Do you remember yourself as a child, playing out who you wanted to be when you grew up? If you haven't become what you've dreamed about or just aren't satisfied with where you are, don't give up; don't *ever* give up!

Once you realize the potential inside you and learn to embrace it, you begin to manifest it.

Chapter 9 – Manifest Magnificence

On the other hand, when you give up on the dream, you dim the light. Along with the ability to manifest greatness, you can also manifest weakness. Our weaknesses can highlight our strengths, but if we don't learn the lesson and turn it around in the next moment in which it presents itself, it can manifest and turn us into victims of circumstance.

Think about turning on a light in a dark room compared to turning on a light in a room brightly lit by the sun. The light bulb in the dark room appears much brighter than in a room that's already lit. You can appreciate its strength in the darkness and its purpose. A lesson is learned when we trip in the dark and realize if we had turned on the light, we wouldn't have tripped in the first place. If you continue to enter this room in the dark and continue to trip and injure yourself, you become a victim of a vicious cycle.

I have the greatest job in the world. Currently, I coach entrepreneurs and help people realize they, too, are extraordinary. When I began my first career as a hairstylist, I felt that was the greatest job in the world, too. I said it again when I changed careers and became a graphic designer, then again when I developed web sites and again when I helped Fortune 100 and 500 companies manage their digital marketing campaigns. Funny thing, though; I never dreamed of or wished for any of these careers as a young child. I dreamed of myself as someone great, talking to and helping people in a public setting. Weird, but true.

Chapter 9 – Manifest Magnificence

And now I realize that if I had not taken this path, I wouldn't be where I am now, public speaking and helping others.

It takes two things to be great in your career: joy and passion. You have to love what you do and always follow your passion. If I hadn't pushed myself out of my comfort zone to focus on each career and be the best at what I did, I never would have manifested the most relevant dream, which has brought me to where I am today. I've seen so many people take shortcuts in hopes of getting to the top. Don't shoot for the top; shoot for magnificence! Be magnificent at whatever you do!

Whenever I read a story about someone who made it to the top, I ask the unanswered question: how happy was this person? They may talk about the awards and accolades by their peers or the riches and fame, but what I want to know is, are they happy? I pinch myself from time to time and say how did I end up being so happy? I made it happen… without even realizing I made it happen. At one moment in time, I simply stepped outside myself and realized I wasn't ordinary, I was extraordinary. I realized I had found the secret and was tapping it again and again. This doesn't mean I haven't had my share of bad luck, challenges and hard times. But I truly believe that all of those experiences helped me to manifest my dreams.

I grew up in the small town of Swartz Creek, just outside Flint, Michigan, the home of General Motors.

Chapter 9 – Manifest Magnificence

I grew up in middle-class America, by every sense of that hyphenated word. It was a good life. My entire family worked for General Motors - grandparents, parents, uncles, aunts and cousins. Both parents usually worked where I grew up, and most of my friends were raised with dual, auto plant incomes. We referred to the company as "Generous Motors" because of the life, income and benefits it provided for our families. It was the world's largest corporation. Today, the title of "world's largest" seems insignificant in comparison to how many other companies are on the heels to be the next biggest corporation and how the title can be passed almost daily from one company to the next. Even as a young girl, "the world's largest corporation" meant very little to me. It was the beginning of what we now refer to as simply the "corporate world." While I can appreciate the impact of its pioneering spirit in today's society, the life I experienced would shape and condition my thinking about corporations. This would define the good, the bad and the ugly truth for me in my corporate journey.

I was conditioned to believe that any car I owned must come from the factory that fed me my entire life. I also listened to my parents complain about the long work hours and bureaucracy, and watched my mother struggle to make it in a man's world. I learned about the words *nepotism, sexual harassment* and *company loyalty*. As I got closer to high school graduation, being part of the corporate world was the furthest thing from my mind.

Chapter 9 – Manifest Magnificence

In the early 80s, "company loyalty" quickly began to lose its meaning as GM began to shut down operations in Flint, Michigan to seek bigger profit margins. I watched as family members and friends lost their jobs and had no other skills to start over again. All they knew was how to work an assembly line. Those skills were exclusive to factory jobs and without a factory, there were no jobs. Those fortunate to keep their jobs watched in disbelief and sadness as their family members and friends were permanently sent home.

I, however, was smart; well, at least I thought I was. I chose not to follow my family members in the auto industry. I went to cosmetology school thinking everyone needs a haircut, especially factory workers. Businesses were open 24/7 to accommodate the day and night shifts of the factories. I was certain I would be safe from the fallout ... until I was involved in a motorcycle accident while vacationing in Daytona Beach, Florida.

This would be the third time I survived a horrific vehicle accident. In my senior year of high school, I survived a head-on collision sitting in the front passenger seat... without a seatbelt. Out of seven people in two vehicles I was the only one able to escape with just a few injuries. Both cars were so mangled no one believed anyone survived. Fortunately, the other six passengers did, but were badly injured, including my brother who was in a coma for a week, with a punctured lung and injured hip that required a replacement in later years.

Chapter 9 – Manifest Magnificence

I was told the young girl in the other car, who sat in the same position I sat in, was paralyzed for life. These moments in time caused me to reflect on the meaning of life and my purpose. Why did I survive? These thoughts pierced my soul and made me who I am today. I live every day with purpose and deep gratitude for being a survivor. These two intentions: purpose and gratitude, illuminate light, and people are drawn to my light. It took many years for me to make these analogies and connections.

Years later, while on vacation in Florida, I knew it was a huge mistake to get on the back of a motorcycle. The mistake was that I went against my gut intuition. Since my earlier accidents, I hated all vehicles and motorcycles were at the top of the list. At first, I refused to ride on it, but I had been convinced it was a short, safe ride to where we were going until a car crossed into our lane to pull into a 7-Eleven.

My leg was crushed and had been almost completely severed at the knee. I spent six weeks in a hospital all alone, my family thousands of miles away. I was an adult and capable of being on my own, but I was desperate to be with my family during this crisis. There was no Family Care Act back then and my family needed to work to survive. It's times like these that your life can turn upside down and you either get swallowed up by the darkness or you chose to turn on the light and make the best of it. I was always the type of person to turn the light on. I kept my parents from worrying by telling them I was fine, and I believed it.

Chapter 9 – Manifest Magnificence

I never doubted for one minute that I would walk out of that hospital whole again.

One day I was scheduled for surgery where they had to remove the dead tissue that had turned black. I had to sign a waiver stating if my leg was badly infected and irreparable, it would have to be amputated. I was not going to let that happen. My mind would not allow me to think about such a loss. The mind is a very powerful tool. It can create miracles. It can also prevent a miracle from happening. I came out of surgery with two legs and went through several skin grafts afterwards. My leg looked like raw meat. You can only imagine how horrified I was when they removed the bandages. But I was determined to be whole again.

I was not fully aware of my injuries until I was released from the hospital in Florida and sought medical attention back in Michigan. I was told my career as a stylist was over, as I would not be able to stand on my leg all day in a physically demanding career. Instead of listening and accepting that, I spent the next 11 years working as a hairstylist, intentionally in denial of having any physical limitations. I eventually became an independent contractor in salons, working for myself. I also contracted with Farouk Shami, the creator of Chi Hair products and also famous for working with Donald Trump on *"The Celebrity Apprentice."* It was HUGE!

I had the opportunity to work on cutting-edge hair coloring techniques on models with Farouk and other international

Chapter 9 – Manifest Magnificence

hairstylists, moving on to teach these techniques in salons throughout Arizona. As an expert hair colorist, a salon owner recommended I learn how to paint to increase my knowledge of color and enhance my hair coloring skills. Eventually, this led me to graphic design school where once again I took myself out of my comfort zone to learn something new - and I loved it!

After graduating, I was asked to return and teach desktop publishing software for a semester before the school eventually helped me find a job as graphic designer for one of the largest credit unions in Arizona. The credit union was the perfect transition from an entrepreneur into the corporate world. I was a struggling single mom at the time and needed a good, stable income with benefits. Since the credit union was a nonprofit institution, working there significantly lowered the competitive pressures and demands. The same demands that many large corporations thrive on that had turned me off to corporate America so long ago. In my eleven years working in the financial industry, I learned a wealth of information about finances and how to market financial services and products. I published a monthly newsletter to 52,000 members a month. I also learned a great deal about cooperation in business. Since credit unions are not-for-profit, we worked alongside other credit unions, sharing marketing materials and ideas, in other words, "the secret sauce" of success. That's something you would never see in for-profit financial institutions such

Chapter 9 – Manifest Magnificence

as banks that compete with one another. Although I knew it was not a typical business model, I felt it was possible such cooperation would carry over into any job. I was certain this type of work ethic, knowledge and information sharing would be embraced by others. I was wrong.

This became a huge challenge in the job market when I changed jobs again to manage a website for an international corporation during the recession years in the mid-2000s. Things were truly ugly in the work force, and once again I was experiencing how morale and loyalty can be destroyed in a business. In fear of being laid off, colleagues did not willingly share their "intellectual property" and expertise. Their strategy was to help the company make the bread without giving away their "secret sauce." Believing such insanity meant job security and would make them irreplaceable. How could they train someone to take on your job responsibilities if no one knew what you actually did? Such attitudes are detrimental in business and I'm not proud to admit that when I realized I could no longer afford to work for the company and decided to leave, I withheld much of my own secret sauce. I felt I wasn't obligated to share it, so I wasn't about to give it away. But this was not who I really was; this was a result of a toxic work environment. It made me realize if you're not part of the solution, you're part of the problem.

When I left that company, I moved into the biggest challenge of my career working for a marketing agency serving Fortune

Chapter 9 – Manifest Magnificence

100 and 500 clients. I worked hard and managed one of my department's biggest client. The client, however, decided to take the secret sauce that we shared with them and move it in-house, cutting back on our services. Shortly thereafter, I was laid off along with 25 percent of the department.

As I look back on all my careers and where I am now, I wonder what my life would look like if I hadn't experienced all the drama and challenges I endured. I wouldn't be the same person. So what have I learned from these experiences? I have learned to become the observer in my life, allowing it to ebb and flow. I have learned to embrace my story and my life and give gratitude. I am humbled by the experiences and people I've engaged with, some whom I've loved and others not so much. The key is to know that they were all relevant in the story of my life, so I must give gratitude to those who played with me and against me. When you learn to embrace the challenges in life and understand this is part of the plan, you find gratitude for those lessons and outcomes. You will, as I did, finally grasp the meaning of life.

My best advice is to focus on being the person you want to work alongside and call on in the future for wisdom and advice. Be kind, respectful of others, even if you don't see eye to eye. If you follow that code of ethics, you will thrive!

Back in my stylist days, I was once fired by the owner of a salon because she felt we had a personality conflict. I was devastated. Me - A personality conflict?

Chapter 9 – Manifest Magnificence

I get along with everybody. But that taught me another important life lesson: not to take anything personally. Shortly thereafter it became obvious this was her problem, not mine.

In the salon business, when you leave you take your clientele with you. After I was fired, several months later, two of the top earning stylists at the same salon heard I was earning a higher commission at my new place of business. Even though they had worked for the owner who had fired me for many years and had built a solid following of clients, they jumped ship because they no longer trusted this woman after she let me go due to her "personal issues." When they realized they would make more money where I was working, they left the salon and took their clientele with them.

Fast forward to more recent years. After being laid off from my last corporate job, I decided it was time to focus on giving back and sharing my knowledge, intellectual property and secret sauce. My purpose is to help others find their true meaning in life, to find joy and peace, and to be magnificent. I can help you find your passion in life and turn it into an online business. The success people are experiencing online is beyond expectations, and there's plenty to go around. What many don't understand is that you can turn any passion into an online business. The Internet today has tested and tried the strategies that work; you just need the right tools and a solid plan. That's what I do! I help you take your passion, set goals, provide the resources and tools to turn it into an online business.

Chapter 9 – Manifest Magnificence

It's easy. The first step is to take each moment and make it count! Embrace it - the good, the bad and the ugly. Focus on turning the lemons into lemonade, taking on every challenge and owning it. So get out of your comfort zone! I want to help you find the extraordinary in your life and to be magnificent! When you find it and live it, you have cracked the code on HAPPY!

- Melody Tune

Chapter 9 – Manifest Magnificence

About The Author – Melody Tune

Melody Tune is the founder and strategic leader at DesignWrx Digital Marketing – DesignWrx.com

A Certified Ziglar Legacy Coach and motivational speaker who shares inspiration and 20 years of digital marketing experience and she has owned over 100 websites. She has helped individuals, sales teams, and organizations to succeed with their digital marketing efforts. She worked with Fortune 100 and 500 clients and currently helps entrepreneurs get started or move to the next level with online branding, blogs and websites. As a former graphic designer, she has a keen eye for visual communications and strategies that work!

Follow Melody on Twitter @melodytune and join her on Facebook: Melody Tune - Ziglar Certified Coach

Chapter 9 – Manifest Magnificence

Life Builders, Stories That Inspire

Life Builders, Stories That Inspire

EPILOGUE

Throughout my life, I have always felt a bigger and better purpose for my life, but I have not always been in pursuit of it, mostly because I have been my own biggest obstacle. I was often distracted by my current comfort zones through my current routines. They kept me from stepping into my full potential and kept me as a prisoner to my routines. I knew that I wanted to "build a better life," I was just not focused enough to see it or empowered enough to make a change.

After years of very strong feelings that God had something better for me, I only took action to start building my life, when I chose to be aware of and act on God's plan for me. I knew this was the only way to fix my life.

Through His grace, I am a new man. I understand my purpose and I am full of life. I can see Him clearly, and I am stronger than ever.

With regard to success, I have always felt that my purpose was to help others through the gift of speaking. I have always dreamed of becoming a motivational/inspirational speaker, but for the largest part of my life, I only considered this a dream.
Who was I to be a speaker?
What credentials or gifts did I have?
These were negative thoughts that I burdened myself with.

So, who am I?
I am a son of our King.
I know Him and He knows me.

Today, all because of Him, and through my obedience to decide, take action and build my life, I am living my life's dream. I am pursuing my life's goal, and most importantly, my life's purpose to help others build their lives.

Believe in God and His plan for your life. Have faith and take action. You too can build your life and make all of your dreams come true because you are also the son or daughter of the same King!

Now Go Forth and Make YOUR Life Exceptional!

- **Mike Rodriguez**

About Mike Rodriguez

Mike Rodriguez is CEO of Mike Rodriguez International, a professional speaking, training and consulting firm. Besides being an author, he is a world-renowned motivator and a leadership and sales expert. Mike is also a former showcase speaker with the world famous Zig Ziglar Corporation and was selected as their speaker and sales expert for the 2015 Ziglar U.S. Tour.

Mike delivers performance-based seminars and trainings and has authored several books which have been promoted by Barnes & Noble. He has been featured on CBS, U.S. News and World Report and has lectured at Baylor University, UNT and K-State Research. His clients include names like Hilton and the Federal Government. As a sales expert, Mike has trained thousands.

Everyone faces challenges; Mike believes that through faith and action, you can overcome the challenges in your life to attain your goals and become who you truly want to be.
He is a high-energy leader who worked in corporate America for two decades training, building, mentoring, and developing top performing people and teams. Mike started as a struggling sales representative, with no experience or formal training. He worked his way up to become a top-performer and an award-winning sales leader. He has held a variety of positions including Director of Sales, Vice-President of Sales, and President/Founder of his own company as a business partner with Southwestern Bell (now AT&T).

Mike has won Chairman's Club Awards, Achiever's Club Awards, Manager of the Year, and numerous vacation trips. He credits his faith, having a plan, taking action, and never giving up for enabling him to prevail over many failures and adversities in his own life. Most importantly, he has always believed in his God-given potential.

Throughout his career, Mike has built productivity-driven training programs and managed multi-million dollar quotas. He has experience delivering powerful messages and creating personal development strategies for new and tenured companies and teams across many industries.

Mike has been happily married since 1991 to the love of his life, and together they have five beautiful daughters. He believes if you have the right attitude, you can have the right kind of success, regardless of the type of industry that you are in.

Life Builders, Stories That Inspire

As a world-renowned speaker,
Mike has experience working with people
from all walks of life.

You can schedule Mike Rodriguez
to speak or train at your next event.
Go to:
www.MikeRodriguezInternational.com

Other books available by Mike Rodriguez:

Finding Your WHY

8 Keys to Exceptional Selling

Break Your Routines to Fix Your Life

M.A.P. Selling

Lion Leadership

Life Builders, Stories That Inspire

Disclaimer & Copyright Information

Some of the events, locales, and conversations have been recreated from memories. In order to maintain their anonymity, in some instances, the names of individuals and places have been changed. As such, some identifying characteristics and details may have changed.

Although the authors and publishers have made every effort to ensure that the information in this book was correct at press time, the authors and publishers do not assume and hereby disclaim any liability to any party for any loss, damage, or disruption caused by errors or omissions, whether such errors or omissions result from negligence, accident, or any other cause.

All quotes, unless otherwise noted,
are attributed to the respective Authors.

Cover illustration, book design and production
Copyright © 2016 by Mike Rodriguez International
www.TributePublishing.com

"Go Forth and Make Your Life Exceptional" ™
and "Go Forth and Sell Something!" ™
are copyrighted trademarks of the Author, Mike Rodriguez.

Scripture references are copyrighted by www.BibleGateway.com
which is operated by the Zondervan Corporation, L.L.C

Life Builders, Stories That Inspire

*"I can do ALL THINGS through Christ
who strengthens me."
Philippians 4:13*

Life Builders, Stories That Inspire

NOTES

NOTES

www.ingramcontent.com/pod-product-compliance
Lightning Source LLC
Chambersburg PA
CBHW021128300426
44113CB00006B/334